Epidemic Subjects—Radical Ontology

Epidemic Subjects—Radical Ontology

Edited by
Elisabeth von Samsonow

diaphanes

This publication was made possible thanks to the generous support of

] a [akademie der bildenden künste wien

Gesellschaft der Freunde
der bildenden Künste

First Edition
ISBN 978-3-03734-596-2
© diaphanes, Zürich-Berlin 2017

Prepress: 2edit, Zürich
Printed in Germany

www.diaphanes.com

Table of Contents

Elisabeth von Samsonow
Epidemic Subjects   7

Suzana Milevska
Becoming-Girl:
Compossibility, Intersectionality, and Agency   13

Levi R. Bryant
Two Ontologies:
Posthumanism and Lacan's Graph of Sexuation   29

Arantzazu Saratxaga Arregi
Girl:
A Paradigmatic Example of Evolutionary Disobedience   51

Boyan Manchev
Pandora's Toys, or zoon technicon
and the Technical Ghosts of the Future   67

Peter Sloterdijk
Theory of Evolution   81

Karin Ferrari
Weird Wired Viral: A Graphic Novel   89

Francesca Coin
Tearing the Neoliberal Subject   99

Johanna Braun
The American Girl and the Horror of (In)Justice   119

Angela Melitopoulos
Autism and Networks   135

Elisabeth von Samsonow
Latency: Biography of an Omniscient Spy   149

Contributors   165

Elisabeth von Samsonow

Epidemic Subjects

This book comprises a series of texts dealing with large-scale shifts within the concept of SUBjectivity—or, more specifically, with its implosion, its revisions and re-inventions. Following the trajectories of SUB, POST, SUPER, SYN, TRANS, and INTER, the contributors examine vertical and horizontal ontologies in recent philosophy and literature as well as their dissolutions, retro-dynamics, and utopias. The crisis of subjectivity parallels the crisis of sovereignty, collectivity, and nationality, which are all swallowed up by certain tendencies in religious and political fundamentalism and terrorism, by scientific hegemony in neuroscience, biotechnologies, and *porno-pharmacology*, by economic crashes, pressures and hypes, and by the use and abuse of media. The book is placed exactly at the epochal rupture where the authoritarian legitimation of identity, cognition, and power is definitively dissolved or questioned, leaving a vacuum to be filled with new proposals, models, and projects. So where to start? Perhaps with a type of subjectivity that is as flat and inclusive as possible, yet clearly defined and productive. Gilles Deleuze and Félix Guattari's concept of *becoming-girl* serves as a common ground or starting point, as it was proposed and developed by these thinkers as an operator of transgressive ontology. "She never ceases to roam upon a body without organs. [... Girls] slip in everywhere, between orders, acts, ages, sexes; they produce *n* molecular sexes on the line of flight in relation to the dualism machines they cross right through."[1] Evidently, the crisis of subjectivity of a type of subjectivity that is in a constant state of crisis—that which has been coded as *the girl*.

This book is obviously different from research concerning the *girl* in pop culture, migration or *brand gestalt*.[2] The theoretical *girlism* of this book explores those dialectic and ultimately aporetic qualities of

---

1   Gilles Deleuze and Félix Guattari, *A Thousand Plateaus: Capitalism and Schizophrenia*, trans. Brian Massumi (Minneapolis, Minn.: University of Minnesota Press, 1987), p. 276–277.
2   In recent years, a number of books focusing on this perspective have been published, such as Susan Hopkins, *Girl Heroes: The New Force in Popular Culture* (Sidney: Pluto Press, 2002); Anita Harris, ed., *All About the Girl: Culture, Power, Identity* (London: Routledge, 2004); The Modern Girl Research Group, ed., *The Modern Girl around the World: Consumption, Modernity and Globalization* (Durham, N.C.: Duke University Press, 2008).

feminist positions that are neither resolved in sociological, multicultural or psychological girl studies, nor via the techno-feminist promotion of implicit modules of self-abolition. This book seeks to gradually dissect the point from which aporetic lines emanate and to subsequently detect, decode, and analyze the flow patterns (see the text by Levi Bryant). Its contributors study emergent symptomatic forms of the radical impossibility of simultaneous identity and assimilation, of growing or becoming and geo- and techno-topological multiplicity, of "national" and *epidemic* subjectivity. Ultimately, the goal is to sketch the anthropo-logics of forces and, respectively, to sketch the logic of a *fluidity of states*, descriptions of which have thus far not appeared on the major sites of philosophy, a fact that has prevented philosophy—intricate and split up into camps though it may otherwise be—from completing the immanent paradigm shift in the regimes of subjectivity.

As opposed to a large portion of contemporary debates, this book places emphasis on the indissoluble connection between ontology as a philosophical basis and subjectivity as a framework for understanding, perception, and *life* in the biopolitical sense. It attempts to explore this connection in manifold facets by contemporary means. Scholars have made a habit of betting on only one horse. However, the crisis of the contemporary subject as diagnosed in this book does not stem from a disjunction of ontology and subjectivity—which is primarily the argument of Speculative Realism, a discipline that switches exclusively to ontology—but instead is a product of the extreme difficulties resulting from philosophical *conjunction*.

In some ways similar to the crisis of basic principles that in the late nineteenth century was generated by the task of reconciling thought with both its historicity and its biological determinism, today's goal is to expand the production of subjectivities not only with logics, economics, politics, gender, and media, but also with planetary types of subjectivity which abandon the capitalist notion of the "global" as a market. The tensions this task creates are enormous. Emerging aporetic tendencies are projected on a tableau that blends cognitive logics with migration politics, gender topics with economy, metaphysics with psychoanalysis, and logic with ideology in such a way as to minimize the danger of confusion. This *fluid* strategy expands the scope of subject-philosophical and subject-political registers considerably and, at the same time, updates the productive approaches introduced in Ian Buchanan and Claire Coleman's book *Deleuze and Feminism* with the Deleuzian adage of *becoming-girl* potentially acting in terms of both exploring and outperforming apories (see the essay by Suzana Milevska).

When the goal is to avoid dialectic games and reciprocal exclusions, the one who always escapes ultimately becomes the expert. Deleuze and Guattari therefore bet on the girl, because she *escapes*. She escapes family as much as she escapes the territory; she escapes sexuality as much as she escapes psychoanalysis,[3] even if Tiqqun accuses her of simple prostitution due to her constant willingness to collaborate.[4] The epidemic subject does not blow its own horn for its relentless competence but does so only when its time has come. Whenever the girl turns around and goes back *into the house*; her arrival then becomes a *haunting* (see the essay by Johanna Braun).

For this reason, the concept of the *epidemic* seemed extraordinarily useful for a new type of subjectivity that structurally corresponds with the *girl*. Lars von Trier beautifully summed up the *epidemic* in his eponymous film from 1987. The quality of the epidemic comprises an activity that expands or travels/wanders, leaves the *narrow abode of the demos*, embarks on a search, goes into hiding. It is placeless, not in its place, active beyond its place. It is the *subject doing field work*. It is necessarily xenophilic. It is as paripinnate as it is antagonistic towards patriarchy and capitalism, which is itself epidemic and therefore *rampant*, highly contagious but different. The *epidemic girl* is an expression of a strange non-manifestation, a form of latency in opposition to the expressive full-onset capitalism and its type of epidemic. On her excursions, the *epidemic girl* makes sure that capitalism, albeit manifest, remains incomplete and only temporarily absolute— that is to say, in a certain sense she is also spectacularly *precarious*. She is the symptom surface of immanent obsolescence, as she—in protuberance—knows more than herself. To the same extent that after each collapse, no matter how disquieting, capitalism and the associated patriarchy—as phantasmatic as they are real—repair themselves, regenerate, and accelerate like a Hydra, the girl and all things associated with her will always remain incomplete and *off*. All the remarkable feminist attempts to put an end to this game have been virtually unable to do any harm (see the essay by Peter Sloterdijk).

It is useless to prescribe to feminism new assimilation guidelines for changing circumstances—in the sense of a competitive neo-pseudo-anti-patriarchalization. It is equally useless to do away with feminism

---

3 Catherine Driscoll, "The Woman in Process: Deleuze, Kristeva and Feminism," in: Ian Buchanan and Claire Colebrook, eds., *Deleuze and Feminist Theory* (Edinburgh: Edinburgh University Press, 2000), p. 73.

4 "The Young-Girl reduces all grandeur to the level of her ass." Tiqqun, *Preliminary Materials for a Theory of the Young-Girl* (Los Angeles, CA: Semiotext(e), 2012), p. 15.

altogether. Quite obviously, feminism is a work in progress—not because it administrates a defect, but because feminism's terminological work contributes significantly to the project of new subjectivities, as Deleuze and Guattari have lucidly recognized.

The new forms of epidemic dialectics are no longer thesis, antithesis, and synthesis, but escape, internment, tunneling, and assimilation. The level on which the migration takes place is indeed, as Deleuze and Guattari have posited, a *body without organs*. However, it is not merely some metamorphic, stem-cell-like entity, but the body of Earth itself which as a point of reference and source has made a pact with the body of the girl, who, in turn, is nothing but a transversality. It seems as if the epidemic subject is the subsidiary of an expanded subjectivity, which is hardly compatible with the spelled-out/manifest subject. Latency secures the perimeter in which the epidemic subject is building on an unknown complicity (see the essay by Angela Melitopoulos).[5] The epidemic subject is a threshold, but, provided that it is an escape, it is also an invitation.

Therefore, although she is not territorial, the girl is a territorializing machine in a completely new sense. As an epiphenomenon, her protuberant body foresees the territorial system, which is to say it foresees Terra, Earth, Gaia, the Unknown.[6] For reasons that have not yet fully unfolded, the girl is on Earth's side, much like she subscribes to exo-partners without actually being able to derive a "scientific Earth-thesis" from this alliance. Together, the girl and Earth form a complex that becomes acutely effective as a transformative moment in the philosophical politics of subjectivity (see my essay).

The girl is technological by way of herself; she is (latently) a virtual production site and, by means of her technology—which, for one, is identical with a theoretical and practical physics and biology that barely registers—she is *erotic* (see the essay by Arantzazu Saratxaga Arregi).

The difficulty of neither letting the ANTI or SUB positions of the girl congeal in substantial subalternity, nor reversing them into triumphant resentment, is resolved to the extent that the complicit subject—Earth as a representative of all exo-partners—makes both itself and the co-

---

5 See also Reza Negarestani, *Cyclonopedia. Complicity with Anonymous Material* (Victoria: Re-Press, 2008).

6 "Echoing a point made by others, I suggest that our incomplete knowledge also means that we should proceed with extreme caution rather that with recklessness in terms of impacts on the Earth's environment." Toby Tyrrell, *On Gaia: A Critical Investigation of the Relationship between Life and Earth* (Princeton, N.J.: Princeton University Press, 2013), p. 217.

implication visible. Gradually, this results in a scene in which the soft or latent forms of subjectivity emerge from the shadows and get *backing*. Horizons shift in a sweeping manner, which is a prerequisite for the possibility of a *radical ecology*.[7] Mick Smith argues that the sovereign state cannot simultaneously have *ecological* sovereignty, since it has only used and exploited nature, which means that even under different pretenses a *state ecology* would amount to the same thing.[8] The epidemic subject specializes in all kinds of self-appointments, and, in a certain anti-sovereign way, it is a sovereign by simple being. From a philosophical perspective, this form of non-state sovereignty is quite attractive. Without it, no awareness, no self-reflection, no thought, no perception, no truth.

Privileging the subaltern, whose contradiction is what Deleuze and Guattari's concept of *becoming-woman* and *becoming-girl* amounts to, in no way serves to sustain with ever more artful means the division of social surfaces, from which capitalist economy profits, even though such a misunderstanding would not be particularly far-fetched (see the essay by Francesca Coin). The level of latency to which the girl belongs is the level that steers the emergences. Even the link between latency and the girl that Sigmund Freud proposed in the psychoanalysis of puberty, bears explosive material, since, according to Freud, suspended sexuality becomes technical, which is to say it becomes a poetic complex and puberty's tinkering box. Latency means that although something is not immediately visible, it is there and has agency. The certain involution which is part of the girl marks the zone of inexhaustible becoming – a competency that defines epidemic dialectics. Here, instead of the clash of cultures, transversality is foreseen, a mysterious way of being constantly (re)born into the world.

The de-domestication that the epidemic subject aims for also has to do with the fact that, as a somewhat baffled Claude Lévi-Strauss notes, "the sexual code [in the myths discussed by C.L.S.] should be apparent only it its masculine references [...]. When the references are feminine, the sexual code becomes latent and is concealed beneath the alimentary code."[9] Beyond the socially and politically virulent totemic functions that casting the female sexual code with the *nourishment*

---

7   See Mick Smith, *Against Ecological Sovereignty: Ethics, Biopolitics, and Saving the Natural World* (Minneapolis, MN: University of Minnesota Press, 2011), pp. 65–100.

8   Ibid, pp. 198–199.

9   Claude Lévi-Strauss quoted in Nicole Shukin, "Deleuze and Feminisms: Involuntary Regulators and Affective Inhibitors," in: Buchanan and Colebrook, eds., *Deleuze and Feminist Theory*, p. 147.

code displays, the latency of the female is, not least, a clue to its trans-human and thereafter consistently post-human radiation. The *nourishment code* that epidemic subjects today interpret with imaginative episodes of binge eating, eating disorders and diets has already become a negative symptom of the coming universal ecology.

I thank the Academy of Fine Arts, which in 2013 in cooperation with the Vienna Art Week (curated by Robert Punkenhofer) hosted the conference *The Girl on Subject: Radical Ontologies*, for supporting this publication. My thanks also go to the Society of Friends of the Fine Arts, Sylvia Eisenburger-Kunz, for subsidizing the printing costs. And, most importantly, I am grateful to all contributors for confronting a question to which there are no simple answers.

Translated by Georg Bauer

Suzana Milevska

Becoming-Girl:
Compossibility, Intersectionality, and Agency

The ways in which feminists have been reading Gilles Deleuze and Félix Guattari's concept of *becoming* have been mostly limited to a specific version of psychoanalysis. Current discussions point out the inadequacy of psychoanalytic critical discourse to grasp the complexity of intersectionality between gender, sexuality, class, and race, as it hinders the agency of criss-crossing these borders.[1] Moreover, the criticism, or even complete refutation, of the concept of *becoming-woman* is mainly determined by the inner contradiction between feminism and psychoanalysis, between striving for a change in the patriarchal order implied by feminist thinking and the fixed and predestined symbolic order as proposed in psychoanalysis. However, the critical feminist approach towards the work of Deleuze and Guattari has shifted and has been enriched by a complex and reflective interest in their concepts of rhizome, desire, event, and assemblage, all of which seem to resonate with contemporary interests in the intersectionality of gender, sexuality, race, and class.

In fact, the most important aspect and contribution of the concept of *becoming-girl* as coined by Deleuze and Guattari in their *Thousand Plateaus* is that it resists the ambivalence of intersectionality pointed out by many vigilant writers. I therefore want to put the emphasis on the complex and anticipatory concept of *becoming-girl* and to contextualize it within more recent discourses, of course with all necessary resonances and distinctions.[2]

This chapter aims to examine the notion of *becoming-girl* from a contemporary feminist perspective and to address and contextualize both its feminist critique and the possible positive feminist use in determined psychoanalytic interpretation. I assume that any feminist criticism of Deleuze and Guattari's understanding of *molar/molecular*

---

1 Compare Kimberlé Crenshaw, "Demarginalizing the Intersection of Race and Sex: A Black Feminist Critique of Antidiscrimination Doctrine, Feminist Theory and Anti-racist Politics," *University of Chicago Legal Forum* 140 (1989): p. 139–167.
2 Compare Gilles Deleuze and Félix Guattari, *A Thousand Plateaus: Capitalism and Schizophrenia*, trans. Brian Massumi (Minneapolis, Minn.: University of Minnesota Press), 1987.

needs to be much subtler, and that any conclusive assertions of its feminist value should be carried out in a cautious manner.[3]

I want to argue that the issue of intersectionality was anticipated by the Deleuzian concept of *compossibility* as it encompasses intersectionality, although the ambivalent and contradictory issues within intersectionality cannot be resolved in this register and understanding of the concept of *becoming:*

> The girl is certainly not defined by virginity; she is defined by a relation of movement and rest, speed and slowness, by a combination of atoms, an emission of particles: haecceity. She never ceases to roam upon a body without organs. She is an abstract line, or a line of flight. Thus girls do not belong to an age group, sex, order, or kingdom: they slip in everywhere, between orders, acts, ages, sexes; they produce n molecular sexes on the line of flight in relation to the dualism machines they cross right through.[4]

Between the two radical oppositional feminist readings of *becoming* in *A Thousand Plateaus*, pro or contra its most relevant concept, there is still a space for discussing the subtle intrinsic contradictions within *becoming* without necessarily abandoning their important philosophic thought all together.

The main question linked to this approach of constructive feminist critique would be, *Why do D + G privilege the word woman?*, which has already been asked by Alice Jardine.[5] It is clear that *becoming-woman* has a special place among other *becomings: becoming-minor, becoming-girl, becoming-animal, becoming-child,* and so forth. According to Deleuze and Guattari, all becomings "begin and pass through becoming-woman."[6]

However, according to Dorothea Olkowski, it is not certain whether the introduction of this concept is necessarily privileging.[7] Olkowski points to one of the few concrete claims of Deleuze and Guattari that sound very much as if *becoming-woman* was really central to all

3 Compare Stevie Schmiedel, "With or Without Lacan? Becoming-Woman between the Language of Organs and the Anorganism of Language," *theory@buffalo8* (30 August 2015), accessible at wings.buffalo.edu/theory/archive/t@b8.pdf.

4 Deleuze and Guattari, *A Thousand Plateaus*, p. 298.

5 Compare Alice Jardine, *Gynesis: Configurations of Women and Modernity* (Ithaca, N.Y.: Cornell University Press, 1985), p. 216.

6 Deleuze and Guattari, *A Thousand Plateaus*, p. 277.

7 Compare Dorothea Olkowski. *Gilles Deleuze and the Ruin of Representation* (Berkeley, Calif.: University of California Press, 1999), p. 35.

becomings, quoting, "Woman as a molar entity must become-woman, so that the man also becomes—or can become-woman."[8]

Becoming-woman according to Deleuze and Guattari is something different from the actual molar body of woman. Actually, "all becomings are molecular, including human becomings. Becomings transform themselves or more precisely they entail shifting between two phases or states, which is in itself another state."[9] Deleuze and Guattari distinguish between the molecular becoming-woman and the inscribed body or actualization of the woman's body that is molar, which is usually what creates confusion when trying to understand the concept of becoming-girl:

> What we term a molar entity is, for example, the woman as defined by her form, endowed with organs and functions and assigned as a subject. Becoming-woman is not imitating this entity or even transforming oneself into it [...] these indissociable aspects of becoming-woman must first be understood as a function of something else: not imitating or assuming the female form, but emitting particles that enter the relation of movement and rest, or the zone of proximity, of a microfemininity, in other words, that produce in us a molecular woman, create the molecular woman.[10]

The critical point to understand the difference between molar and molecular is thus how *becoming-girl* and *becoming-woman* relate to the reality of the experience and how these two concepts resist phallocentric and schizo-capitalist culture:

In other words, becoming-woman is not learning about our bodies or the inscriptions upon them; becoming-woman does not replicate the reality of our experiences in a phallocentric, capitalist culture. Becoming-woman is what we were never allowed to be before we became inscribed into the culture.[11]

However, it is important to question whether the acknowledgment of the importance of woman and *becoming-woman* is necessarily a privileged position and what it *does* to the rest of the concepts in *A Thousand Plateaus*. It is obvious that the notion of *becoming-woman*, even though it is treated as so important, is closely linked with the other becomings, particularly with *becoming-girl* and *becoming-minor*.

---

8 Deleuze and Guattari, *A Thousand Plateaus*, p. 275–276.
9 Jenny Bay, "Girls and Becoming-Woman," *Vitanza* (E5352, Deleuze & Guattari and Rhetorical Theory), accessible at www.uta.edu/HyperNews/get/delgua/46. html.
10 Deleuze and Guattari, *A Thousand Plateaus*, p. 275.
11 Jenny Bay, "Girls and Becoming-Woman."

Becoming-Girl: Stealing the Body, Not Owning It

The issue of becoming-girl is all about the body but not about owning the body: According to Deleuze and Guattari becoming-girl is rather about stealing, or even hijacking *girl's becoming*:

> The girl's becoming is stolen first, in order to impose a history, or prehistory, upon her. The boy's turn comes next, but it is by using the girl as an example, by pointing to the girl as the object of his desire, that an opposed organism, a dominant history is fabricated for him too. The girl is the first victim, but she must also serve as an example and a trap.[12]

The concept of *body without organs* is contrasted by the "anorganism" of the body, which for Deleuze and Guattari is inseparable from a becoming-woman and subsequently from the production of a molecular woman: "Doubtless, the girl becomes a woman in the molar or organic sense. But conversely, becoming-woman or the molecular woman is the girl herself."[13]

In fact, it is about stealing the body from the girl, not allowing her to *be* with her body: "the girl and child do not become; it is becoming itself that is a girl or child. The child does not become an adult any more than the girl becomes a woman; the girl is the *becoming-woman* of each sex, just as the child is the becoming-young of every age."[14] There is a certain potential of such becoming that may interrupt and disable the vicious circle of the neoliberal libidinal economy that implants the *becoming-girl* as its main victim through slow processes and procedures as hierarchical shaming, exclusion, exposing, and molesting.

But the question is, if becoming-woman is the girl herself, then what comes before the girl, and is there another *becoming* between the *becoming-girl* and *becoming-woman*? One might also think "about the implications of becoming-woman as the key to all becomings—not because of any feminist concerns about the appropriation of women, but because of the prioritizing of one becoming as the base of all becomings, the place where all becomings must come in order to proceed. This assumes that there is a stable point, a stable becoming to which all becoming-moleculars are connected."[15] All this sounds prob-

---

12 Deleuze and Guattari, *A Thousand Plateaus*, p. 297.
13 Ibid., p. 297.
14 Ibid., p. 277.
15 Jenny Bay, "Girls and Becoming-Woman."

lematic, especially when taking into account the Deleuzian insistence on radical singularities.

Becoming-woman turns out to be the one center of all molecular becomings because, "[a]lthough all becomings are already molecular, including becoming woman, it must be said that all becomings begin with and pass through becoming-woman. It is the key to all the other becomings."[16]

According to Jenny Bay, the potential and agency of radical micropolitics is the reason for stripping the girl's body:

> If we think about what might be vibrating between the notions of those becomings and between becoming-woman and the girl, the potential for radical micropolitics may come further to the surface. [With] the inscribing and forcing the girl to conform to accepted norms, her body is stripped of her. At the same time, her becoming—all that she could be on the molecular level—is stripped away from her.[17]

For Bay, becoming the molecular woman is actually becoming-girl. She points out the fact that Deleuze and Guattari never say, "the girl is 'reclaimed' in each of us or that the girl inside of us all is set free."[18] Therefore, this girl represents a special condition that was blocked by the state apparatus, a specific gender that is linked to biology and sexuality. "Sexuality is the production of a thousand sexes, which are so many uncontrollable becomings. Sexuality proceeds by way of the becoming-woman of the man and the becoming-animal of the human: an emission of particles."[19]

Blocking the becoming-girl by hijacking the girl's body is emphasized in neoliberalism as it inconspicuously intervenes in the biopolitical control over the molecular girl's body and becoming-girl. This stresses the anticipatory warnings of Deleuze and Guattari's analysis of schizo-capitalism and its hyper-production of new norms via surveillance and biopower that particularly enforce body images induced by patriarchy. Even if a very carefully crafted discourse suggests a way out, some of these swift interpretations of various new cultural practices as empowering are somewhat uncritical.[20]

---

16 Deleuze and Guattari, *A Thousand Plateaus*, p. 299.
17 Jenny Bay, "Girls and Becoming-Woman."
18 Ibid.
19 Deleuze and Guattari, *A Thousand Plateaus*, p. 300.
20 Compare Gilles Deleuze, "Postscript on the Societies of Control," *October* vol. 59 (Winter 1992), p. 3–7.

Intersectionality and Becoming-Minor

Becoming-minor, to use the Deleuzian concept, is to ditch the inherited position and not only to identify with the position of the other, the weaker or minor identity, but also to foster such an identity by setting an example. According to Deleuze, *becoming-minor* simultaneously needs two different movements: one by which the subject will be withdrawn from the majority, and another by which a new term will rise up from the minority.[21] *Becoming-minor* consists of "double agents," multiplicities that produce each new identity statement so that any individual statement is already marked by the statements of the next "agents," and the process thus builds up to completeness. However, completeness is non-representable.

Deleuze constructs his dialectics around the problem of how to affirm a productive continuity through a search for completeness, whilst also responding to the proposition that continuity is never a matter of identities or representations. In other words, we can never represent or identify continuity, even relatively and in an open-ended transforming way.[22]

Becoming-minor and becoming-girl are closely linked to the issue of the relation between identity and event. Williams emphasizes the relevance of this relation as it is elaborated by Deleuze: "Identities are encountered in events that vary according to a 'drama' of multiple sensations and hence intensities."[23] The final result of these complex physical and linguistic movements is the emergence of a specific *grammar* of the work that locates a certain voice and differentiates between "who is speaking"—which becomes irrelevant—and "the speaking itself."

Claire Colebrook differentiates between the grammar of *being* and the grammar of *becoming* as ways of speaking. At first, she identifies the grammar and logic of the subject as tied to a certain way of speaking:

> The very concept of the subject is tied to a strategy of being and essence, rather than becoming. And this is because the subject is not just a political category or representation but a movement of grammar. The very notion of subject in the grammatical sense, as a being capable of predication, is also tied to a broader notion of grammar whereby political subjects or identities

21 Deleuze and Guattari, *A Thousand Plateaus*, p. 291.
22 James Williams, "Deleuze," University of Dundee, 12 January 2004, last accessed on 10 April 2006, http://www.dundee.ac.uk/philosophy/williams/Deleuze/.
23 Ibid.

are effected through certain ways of speaking. The concept and logic of the subject as such, then, demands or provokes a movement of thought, a specific temporality and, ultimately, a strategy of reactivism, recognition, and being (rather than becoming).[24]

Majoritarianism is affected by becoming-minoritarian, and the mere possibilities of becoming-minoritarian shape majoritarianism. There are many restraints that culture imposes on normal subjectivity in a form of biopower, and these restraints are mainly suspected and disavowed in *becoming*. "Becoming here is a means to get 'outside,' which is perhaps what Deleuze and Guattari meant in their insistence of becoming-woman."[25]

Perhaps Patricia MacCormack identifies the inner contradictions within feminist thought as stemming from the contradictions of humanity and language in all attempts to grasp these relations in global terms:

> However, as feminists know, each discourse of feminism is a multiple proliferation of a variety of discourses. Most of these aim to open discussion, investigating the gaps and holes in the discourse of "humanity," essentially "manity" or more correctly "majoritanity."[26]

Body and Becoming-Subject

Becoming is about negotiating the discursive constitution of the subject, but it should not be forgotten that "[d]iscourse is corporeal because we are enfleshed versions of the speech that constitutes us from culture without and from self-regulation or identification within. [...] In order for there to ever be a potential for actual becoming, the potential of the body we are now must be recognised."[27] The relation between body and subjectivity is established through language and discourse exactly as a becoming that intervenes in subjectivity and de-familiarizes it:

---

24 Claire Colebrook, "A Grammar of Becoming: Strategy, Subjectivism, and Style," in: Elizabeth Grosz, ed., *Becomings—Explorations in Time, Memory, and Futures* (Ithaca, N.Y.: Cornell University Press, 1999), p. 117–118.
25 Patricia MacCormack, "Perversion: Transgressive Sexuality and Becoming-Monster," *thirdspace* 3/2 (March 2004), p. 27–40 (print), 23 pars. (web). 2 April 2006, accessible at http://journals.sfu.ca/thirdspace/index.php/journal/article/viewArticle/maccormack/174
26 Ibid.
27 Ibid.

Becoming is an aspiration for change in thinking the material self. Becoming deterritorialises subjectivity, mobilising rather than reifying the way we think self. The familiar territory of subjectivity resonates with sexual territory but more importantly with the familiar territory of how we think our subjectivity.[28]

Instead of a *subordinate* strategy of the subject, Colebrook calls for a sustained "strategy of becoming."[29] According to Colebrook, "the self it effects is not an essence but an event."[30]

Thus, she obviously objects to any conceptualization of the subject as something fixed and eternally given. Furthermore, following Deleuze, she paraphrases his notion of *becoming*: "Before there is a genesis that can be traced back to an origin or condition, there is a multiple and synchronic stratification and structuring, not something located at a single point but a creation of possible points through the event of lines, striations, and articulations."[31]

This notion of multiplicity that always already stratifies the origin seems to be in direct conflict with the endless quest for the origin of one's own identity. There is only a locating of multiple selves in the rhizome of becomings: "Every thought is already a tribe."[32] *Becoming* in the Deleuzian sense is neither a process that takes place in linear time nor a result of dialectically overcoming certain obstacles or contradictions, but more about *becoming offspring of the event*:

> Nothing more can be said, and no more has ever been said: to become worthy of what happens to us, and thus to will and release the event, to become the offspring of one's own events, and thereby to be reborn, to have one more birth, and to break with one's carnal birth—to become the offspring of one's events and not of one's actions, for the action is itself produced by the offspring of the event.[33]

This idea of becoming *offspring of one's events and not of one's actions* resonates with the Nietzschean concept of the *eternal return* as understood by Deleuze in what he has called *the third figure of transmutation* in the process of becoming:

---

28 Ibid.

29 Colebrook, *A Grammar of Becoming: Strategy, Subjectivism, and Style*, p. 118.

30 Ibid., p. 132.

31 Ibid.

32 Deleuze and Guattari, *A Thousand Plateaus*, p. 377.

33 Deleuze. *The Logic of Sense*, trans. Mark Lester (New York, N.Y.: Columbia University Press), p. 149–150.

Becoming is no longer opposed Being, nor is the multiple opposed to the One (these oppositions being the categories of nihilism). On the contrary, what is affirmed is the One of multiplicity, the Being of becoming [...] We now see what this third figure is: the play of the eternal return. This return is precisely the Being of becoming, the one of multiplicity, the necessity of chance. Thus we must not make of the eternal return a *return of the same*.[34]

Becoming-subject is not about re-creating new identities but more about co-existence and compossibility: expressing the *difference* without overwriting it with solely one language but emphasizing *speaking* itself:

Subjectively, common sense subsumes under itself the various faculties of the soul, or the differentiated organs of the body, and brings them to bear upon a unity which is capable of saying "I." One and the same self perceives, imagines, remembers, knows, etc.; one and the same breathes, sleeps, walks, and eats [...]. Language does not seem possible without this subject which expresses and manifests itself in it, and which says what it does.[35]

This recalls the logic of Gayatri Spivak's notion of subaltern subjects that have special strategies. It also seems slightly different from Judith Butler's notion of the production of subject through subjection to the law[36] and through the process of acquitting oneself from presumed guilt:

To become a "subject" is thus to have been presumed guilty, then tried and declared innocent. Because this declaration is not a single act but a status incessantly *reproduced*, to become a "subject" is to be continuously in the process of acquitting oneself of the accusation of guilt. [...] Yet because this guilt conditions the subject, it constitutes the prehistory of the subjection to the law by which the subject is produced.[37]

---

34 Deleuze, *Pure Immanence: Essays on A Life*, trans. Anne Boyman (New York: Zone Books. 2001), p. 86–87.

35 Deleuze, *The Logic of Sense*, p. 78.

36 Butler's notion of the production of subject is based on Louis Althusser, *Ideology and Ideological State Apparatusses*, in *Lenin and Philosophy and other Essays*, trans. Ben Brewster (New York: Monthly Review Press) 1971, pp. 121–176

37 Judith Butler, *The Psychic Life of Power* (Stanford, Calif.: Stanford University Press, 1997), p. 118.

While for Butler the subject internalizes the assumed guilt before it is even a subject (guilt precedes the subject) and is forced to become a subject in this continuous process of acquitting, Spivak suggests that the process of subjectification is carried on by a subject who tricks the system by using its own means and strategies.[38]

According to Deleuze, *becoming* is not an evolutionary process, something that happens to everybody, but rather a question of *micropolitics:*

> Becoming is a rhizome, not a classificatory or genealogical tree. Becoming is certainly not imitating, or identifying with something; neither is it regressing-progressing; neither is it corresponding, establishing corresponding relations; neither it is producing, producing a filiation or producing through filiation. Becoming is a verb with a consistency all its own; it does not reduce to, or lead back to, "appearing," "being," "equalling," or "producing."[39]

I argue that, aside from the unresolved macropolitics that according to Deleuze and Guattari is the enemy of *becoming*, a discussion of *becoming-woman* is possible in a more general cultural context. *Becoming* can also take place in a macropolitical context, but not as an accumulation of *micro-becomings*. The macropolitics and micropolitics of becoming-girl are the best examples of the impossibility of thinking these two levels of becoming in isolation from one another—they are inextricably intertwined. It is instrumental, however, to remember that micropolitical becoming takes place despite the dominant macropolitics.

In conclusion, I propose another becoming, a *becoming-gender-difference* that is based on Deleuze's notion of *compossible events. Being* is always already grand in scale, and in order to become other, it needs to be deterritorialized. In contrast, *becoming-gender-difference* simultaneously needs the same two movements as becoming-minor: one by which the subject will be isolated from the majority and another by which it will rise up from the minority.[40] The difference between Derridean *différance* and the Deleuzian expression of difference lies in the concept of compossibility that contains a kind of *disjunctive dialectics:*

38 Gayatri Chakravorty Spivak, "Gender—Citizenship—Representation," guest lecture, Academy of Fine Arts, Vienna, 22 May *2014.*
39 Deleuze and Guattari, *A Thousand Plateaus*, p. 239.
40 Compare ibid, p. 291.

The expressed world is made of differential relations and of contiguous singularities. It is formed as a world precisely to the extent that the series which depend on each singularity converge with the series which depend on others. *This convergence defines "compossibility" as a rule of a world synthesis.* Where the series diverge, another world begins, incompossible with the first. The extraordinary notion of compossibility is thus defined as a *continuum* of singularities, whereby continuity has the convergence of series as its ideational criterion. It follows that the notion of incompossibility is not reducible to the notion of contradiction.[41]

According to Deleuze's definition of compossibility, the relation between events cannot be defined as causal and consequential. "Events are never causes of one another, but rather enter the relations of quasi-causality, an unreal and ghostly causality, endlessly reappearing in the two senses."[42] Events can either *co-exist* or are *incompossible*, thus not all events can take place in parallel: "Two events are compossible when the series which are organized around their singularities extend in all directions; they are incompossible when the series diverge in the vicinity of constitutive singularities."[43] The event of *becoming-gender-difference* does not engage in any privileging of *becoming-woman* for the simple reason that instead of appropriating and emphasizing *woman*, it treats *becoming* as compossible events of multiple becomings.

Affirmative Aspects of Becoming, Intersectionality, and Agency

In this context, it is indispensable to look at the potentials of affirmative feminist methodology and epistemology specific to historic and more recent feminist art practice. For too long, feminist theory has been dominated by a negative cognitive logic that originated in psychoanalysis and post-structuralism. Although feminist art has been around for at least half a decade, there has been no substantial reflection on the anticipatory aspects or the specificity of feminist research methods that diverged from Jacques Lacan's symbolic order. I therefore find it productive to explore and appraise the specific affirmative processes

---

41 Deleuze, *The Logic of Sense*, p. 110–111.
42 Ibid, p. 33.
43 Ibid, p. 172.

that have been instigated by feminist theory and argue that they provide a basis for unique artistic thinking.[44]

The theoretical concept of agency, although already present as a term in Michel Foucault's texts, had not been thoroughly developed until the late 1990s. Today it is one of the most relevant theoretical foundations for the recent return of feminist and queer theories to the kind of positive engagement and sociopolitical activism that characterized the early stages of these theoretical movements. Theorists who have an affirmative approach to their work—even if they cannot be characterized as activists in their critique of society—propose specific ways of overcoming societal hierarchies and injustices. While the prevailing constructionist assumptions posit that the subject is always already subsumed under a pre-established symbolic order and constructed around a certain *lack*, my research focuses on visual material that allows for alternative readings of, and ways to overcome, hegemonic regimes of representation.

It was the book *Gender and Agency: Reconfiguring the Subject in Feminist and Social Theory* by Lois McNay and the possibilities offered by the term *agency* that prompted me to further explore the limitations of the psychoanalytical approach in a feminist context.[45] Not all feminists accepted the analytical direction of Judith Butler's constructivist "school."[46] In discussing the crisis in the different regimes of representation and subjectivity, I suggest using the principle of agency as a complementary approach to Deleuze's affirmative concept of *becoming-woman*. In fact, McNay argues that the concept of *lack* is a universal category that confines the theories of subjectification and thus prevents them from providing any narrative for change. Agency, compossibility, transversality, and intersectionality are certain forms of a positive feminist shift that challenges psychoanalysis, the

---

44 Compare Suzana Milevska, *Gender Difference in the Balkans: Archives of Representations of Gender Difference and Agency in Visual Culture and Contemporary Arts in the Balkans* (Saarbrücken: VDM Verlag, 2010). This book was based on my Ph.D. research project at the Visual Cultures Department, Goldsmiths College, University of London, 2001–2006.
45 Compare Lois McNay, *Gender and Agency: Reconfiguring the Subject in Feminist and Social Theory* (Cambridge: Polity Press, 2000), p. 2–3.
46 Compare Nancy Fraser, "The Uses and Abuses of French Discourse Theories for Feminist Politics," in Silvestra Mariniello and Paul A. Bové, eds., *Gendered Agents Women and Institutional Knowledge* (Durham, N.C.: Duke University Press, 1998), p. 123–143; Patricia S. Mann, *Micro-Politics: Agency in a Postfeminist Era* (Minneapolis, Minn.: University of Minnesota Press, 1994); Chandra Talpade Mohanty, *Feminism Without Borders: Decolonizing Theory, Practicing Solidarity* (Durham, N.C.: Duke University Press 2003), fifth ed.

always already determined and predestined patriarchal symbolic order inscribed in the language, and the Law of the Father.[47]

Chandra Talpade Mohanty and Marnia Lazreg carefully discussed the calls against an "essentialism of difference" and proposed a nuanced discussion of the traps of any generalized attacks of either universalist, essentialist, or constructivist feminist theories: "The point is neither to subsume other women under one's own experience nor to uphold a separate truth for them."[48] The model of comparative feminist studies that Mohanty proposes is helpful because it does not focus on any single fixed theory or fixed interpretation of different theories and thus gives more options for grasping the complexities of the gender issue in a globalized world. She reminds us that the relationship between the local and the global is reciprocal; they constitute each other since their relationship is not defined in material ways in terms of physical geography and territories. Instead, she argues, they are linked conceptually, temporally, and contextually.

This kind of comparative framework assumes intersections of race, class, nation, gender, and sexuality, and suggests an analysis of different but intertwining historic experiences of oppression and exploitation. At the same time, it entails an interrogation of the potential for solidarity and mutuality in the struggle, both on specific and universal levels.[49] Therefore, the tasks of feminists should be constantly re-imagined by "transcending the conceptual borders inherent in the old cartographies"[50] and by introducing models of intersecting and transversal research, particularly in the study of different regions and cultures.[51] *Becoming-girl* is one of the concepts that could be most appropriate for such intersectional comparisons. Deleuze and Guattari's original conceptualization proposed it as one of the proofs that symbolic order, regardless of how strongly it was inscribed within different patriarchal cultures, was easy to be transgressed.

Some similar concerns were raised recently by theorists who urged for solidarity and conviviality, or transversality, in cultural and feminist studies in contrast to the prevailing poststructuralist and psychoanalytical theoretical approach that invested too much in the fixed

---

47 Compare Patricia S. Mann, *Micro-Politics*, p. 80–81.
48 Chandra Talpade Mohanty, *Feminism Without Borders*, p. 257.
49 Ibid., p. 241–242.
50 Ella Shohat, "Area Studies, Transnationalism, and the Feminist Production of Knowledge," in *Signs: Journal of Women in Culture and Society*, vol. 26, no. 4 (2001), p. 1269–1272.
51 Compare Mohanty, *Feminism Without Borders*, p. 241; Ella Shohat, "Area Studies."

psychic structures and therefore did not allow for any societal transformations. Lois MacNay's call for diverging from Judith Butler's psychoanalytical negative paradigms, which were "regarded as relatively ahistorical theories of patriarchy and female subordination"[52] is necessary in order to reconceptualize agency, which, in her words, is "often formulated as explanations of how gender identity is a durable but not immutable phenomenon."[53]

The politics of affects is one of the visionary political projects that, according to Eve Kosofsky Sedgwick, Sara Ahmed and others, should emphasize caring for ourselves and embracing solidarity, responsibility, generosity, and reciprocity in order to destabilize gender identity, race, and queer sexuality in the best tradition of affect theory.[54] Other feminists, such as Nira Yuval-Davis and Encarnación Gutiérrez Rodríguez, call for "a new cosmological vision of transversal conviviality, based on the acknowledgment of interconnectedness and interdependency, in short: transversality."[55] In this context it is relevant to stress that intersectionality is not understood as a kind of neutral normative speech, but rather as a call for working through the crossing points of becoming-girl. Becoming-girl is not understood as a mere precursor of becoming-woman but consists of compossible becoming events.

The ambiguous rhetoric of the imagery in historic archives and all too many exclusions from patriarchal regimes of representation in these images, especially in most patriarchal regions, such as the Balkans (e.g., Albania, Kosovo, Monte Negro, Macedonia), give way to arguments that deconstruct the prescriptive and unified understanding of *becoming-girl* and undergird the urgency of discussing the agency of intersectionality and conviviality. The images stored in these clandestine repositories (rarely or never exhibited publically), which are dedicated precisely to guarding and preserving identity and truth, unravel the social potentials for resistance of the *becoming-girl* against

---

52 Lois McNay, *Gender and Agency*, p. 2.
53 Ibid.
54 Compare Eve Kosofsky Sedgwick, *Touching Feeling: Affect, Pedagogy, Performativity* (Durham, N.C.: Duke University Press, 2003) p. 64; Sara Ahmed, "Feminist Killjoys (And Other Wilful Subjects)," in: *The Scholar and Feminist Online*, vol. 8, no.3 (Summer 2010), accessible at http://sfonline.barnard.edu/polyphonic/print_ahmed.htm
55 Encarnación Gutiérrez Rodríguez, "Politics of Affects, Transversal Conviviality," in: transversal: multilingual webjournal, (1/2011), accessible at http://eipcp.net/transversal/0811/gutierrezrodriguez/en; *see also* Nira Yuval-Davis, "What is Transversal Politics," in: *Soundings: A Journal of Politics and Culture*, no. 12 (Summer 1999), p. 94.

the norm in different cultural contexts. Such potentials encompass different anthropological phenomena, images, figures, and events, such as, for instance, photographs of the unveiling of monuments, of young female soldiers, sworn virgins, or socialist revolutionaries.[56] Therefore, one cannot but conclude that as long as one focuses merely on the symbolic order, one runs the risk of overlooking the potentiality of *becoming-girl* that rests with the deconstruction of the predetermined order in the field of the imaginary conceptualization of solidarity, agency, and hope for a patriarchy-less society.

---

56 Milevska, *Gender Difference in the Balkans*, p. 180–185. The central claim in this book is that feminist discourse should examine affirmative ways and processes of constructing new subjectivities, rather than focus merely on subjection and oppression. The book was imagined as a cross-disciplinary archive informed by the overlooked discourses and images of gender difference and agency from the past, and its central aim was to reinterpret them through contemporary works of art: photographs, films, objects, videos, installations, and performances.

Levi R. Bryant

Two Ontologies:
Posthumanism and Lacan's Graph of Sexuation

1.
Humanism, Posthumanism, Structure, and Matheme

Posthumanism calls for a fundamental reconceptualization of ontology, epistemology, ethics, and political theory so as to free these domains from their anthropocentrism and human exceptionalism. Within the context of this essay, I will focus on how ontology must be rethought if it is to be adequate to posthumanism, for ontological assumptions pervade questions of epistemology, ethics, and political theory. My thesis is that a genuinely posthuman ontology must be what I call a *feminine ontology*. At the level of form or structure, it must be an ontology that challenges all logics of sovereignty or, what amounts to the same thing, patriarchy. In this regard, a posthuman ontology must also be an a-theistic ontology; an ontology without fathers, masters, kings, or godheads where *subjects* are always open to a world that exceeds them and where the self is an-other in much the same sense that Stacy Alaimo describes under the title of *trans-corporeality*[1] and Karen Barad names under the title of *intra-action*.[2] In short, a posthumanist ontology would not simply be one that contests all sovereign terms in the name of a flat and anarchic plane of immanent being composed of intra-acting entities; it would also be an ontology that contests the seclusion of the subject, its solipsism or self-mastery, its bounded nature as an entity that remains separated from the world in which it is enmeshed like a little general surveying his soldiers on a hill from afar without being in the battle himself. My argument is that a deviant Deleuzian reading of Lacan's graphs of sexuation can help us to think such an ontology.

Here the question is not one of contesting this or that particular ontology—for example, the ontology of Plato or Heidegger—but rather of contesting a deep structure of ontological thought that has domi-

---

1   See Stacy Alaimo, *Bodily Natures: Science, Environment, and the Material Self* (Bloomington, Ind.: Indiana University Press, 2010).

2   See Karen Barad, *Meeting the Universe Half-Way: Quantum Physics and the Entanglement of Matter and Meaning* (Durham, N.C.: Duke University Press, 2007).

nated Western philosophy for the last twenty-five hundred years and is common to many philosophical orientations despite their differences from one another. While there have been exceptions to this ontological framework—notably Lucretius and Spinoza—I contend that this basic structure has nonetheless dominated philosophical thought and the world of theory.

As Cary Wolfe has noted, *posthumanism* has been a highly contested term, referring to everything from the anti-humanisms of thinkers such as Foucault and Althusser, the trans-humanisms of those who believe that we will move beyond the human through digital technologies that will allow us to surmount our biological limitations through uploading our minds to computers and prosthetically melding ourselves with various technologies, to the work of various critical animal and disability theorists.[3] Here I follow Wolfe in understanding posthumanism to signify 1) a position that "names the embodiment and embeddedness of the human being in not just its biological but also its technological world, the prosthetic coevolution of the human animal with the technicity of tools and external archival mechanisms (such as language and culture),"[4] and that 2) rejects *anthropological universals* and the repression of the animal both with respect to the dimension of our own animality and life beyond the human as well.[5]

Where humanism is premised on the human, "escaping or repressing not just its animal origins in nature, the biological, and the evolutionary, but more generally by transcending the bonds of materiality and embodiment altogether"[6] (the repression of affectivity, embodiment, and embeddedness), an idealized conception of the human in the form of anthropological universals, and human exceptionalism, posthumanism entails a flattening of ontology where humans are no longer understood as sovereigns over all other beings, as the Biblical narrative of Adam in the Garden would have it, but as beings—with their own unique powers and capacities, to be sure—that are *among* other beings, that are inseparable from materiality both in the form of the materiality of the world and in the most intimate recesses of our own being, which opens on to a regard for beings beyond ourselves.

Humanist orientations have had far-reaching ethical and political implications. In the postulation of anthropological universals that are all too often but culturally contingent prejudices, humanism played

---

3 Cary Wolfe, *What is Posthumanism?* (Minneapolis, Minn.: University of Minnesota Press, 2010), p. xi–xiv.

4 Ibid., p. xv.

5 Compare ibid., pp. xvi–xviii.

6 Ibid., p. xv.

a key role in the subjugation and genocide of other cultures in western colonial expansions. It has also played a central role in racisms and sexisms. As Elizabeth Grosz notes, "[p]hilosophy has attributed to man a power that animals lack (and often that women, children, slaves, foreigners, and others lack: the alignment of the most abjected others with animals is ubiquitous)."[7] These same anthropological universals have played a central role in the project of eugenics insofar as the disabled and, in particular, the mentally disabled, have been seen not as beings that inhabit a different universe of experience with different capacities, but as lacking and deficient with respect to the proposed essence of what humans are *supposed* to be. Likewise, the repression of materiality, embodiment, and embeddedness, the characterization of the human as that which transcends all of these things through its rationality, has helped to cultivate an attitude where the natural world is seen as something that is merely there for our exploitation, and where it is far more difficult to think ecologically.

My thesis is that western thought since the Greeks has predominantly been organized around a deep structure that I call *logics of sovereignty* that lies at the core of these humanist orientations. Overcoming humanism entails not simply critiquing this or that humanist thesis, but overcoming this ontological structure of thought. Discerning this requires thinking *structurally*. What does it mean to think structurally? To think structurally is to suspend one's focus on the *content* of a position, instead attending to *relations* between elements. At the level of content, two formations can be quite different, while at the level of structure they can be identical. Take first the example of two houses. Two houses can be different in that one is made of bricks, the other of wood, the walls are painted different colors, one is carpeted, the other is not, and so forth. These houses differ at the level of content. Bricks are a different material than wood. However, these houses can nonetheless be structurally identical in that they share the same floor plan. Despite a difference in materials, one and the same pattern, one and the same set of relations, is instantiated in the materials of these two houses. If we shift from entities like houses to formations like political orders, we can see why thinking structurally is important. If we think at the level of content, for example, we might believe that Margaret Thatcher becoming prime minister is an important feminist revolution. One content, a male, has been replaced by another, a woman. However, if we approach the political order in terms of relations between elements, we might discover that one and the same

---

7   Elizabeth Grosz, *Becoming Undone: Darwinian Reflections on Life, Politics, and Art* (Durham, N.C.: Duke University Press, 2011), p. 12.

order of patriarchy is instantiated in Thatcher's governance. While the person in the leadership role is of a different biological gender (content), she nonetheless occupies a position structurally identical to that of a father or sovereign. Fighting patriarchy would here consist in targeting something more fundamental than the primacy of one biological gender. It would consist in targeting a fundamental *patriarchal structure* that can be instantiated by members of *both* sexes. Thinking structurally about philosophy in relation to posthumanism would here consist in discerning how very divergent ontologies instantiate one and the same structure of humanism and transcendence, rather than focusing on whether, for example, Plato is right in his theory of the forms or Descartes in his account of the subject. Plato and Descartes would be seen to presuppose the same structural ontology, despite the vast differences between the content of their respective positions.

Lacan's mathemes and, in particular, his graph of sexuation provide us with the means for both thinking this structure and a posthumanist alternative. Lacan introduced the matheme, these simple algebraic symbols, as a tool to overcome lures of the imaginary in the psychoanalytic clinic and draw attention to the structural or functional role of elements. What he sought was a formalization of Freud's theory and practice. To see the advantage of mathemes, take the example of the Oedipus complex. If we begin from the standpoint of the imaginary—where, in this case, the imaginary signifies common perceptual images—we might assume that the father that instantiates the prohibition against incest necessarily refers to a male that is the biological father of the child. Such an assumption could potentially have very concrete consequences for what we understand to be going on with respect to our analysands or when we analyze other cultures not based on the nuclear family. Insofar as psychoanalysis holds that the father is necessary for the production of ordinary neurotic subjects, we might be led to believe children raised in single parent families by their mother or children raised by two mothers will necessarily be psychotic or perverse by virtue of a *male* being absent.[8] Likewise, in cultures with kinship structures where a male does not play an immediate role such as the Na of the Chinese highlands,[9] we might be led to believe that these societies will be characterized by psychosis or perversion. Such

---

8 Here I presuppose Lacan's account of the role that the name-of-the-father plays in the structures of neurosis, psychosis, and perversion. For an excellent account of this, compare Bruce Fink, *A Clinical Introduction to Lacanian Psychoanalysis: Theory and Technique* (Cambridge, Mass.: Harvard University Press, 1997).

9 See also Hua Cai, *A Society Without Fathers or Husbands: The Na of China*, trans. Asti Hustvedt (New York, N.Y.: Zone Books, 2001).

conclusions arise from thinking of the paternal function in terms of *images* of the male body. When, however, we think of paternity as a symbolic *function* and replace the term *father* with a matheme or algebraic symbol such as S1, this tendency is diminished, and we can begin to discern how something entirely unrelated to masculine bodies can serve an identical function in our subjective economies. For example, in a couple composed of two women, one of those *women* can serve the function of S1 and instantiate the incest prohibition or signal that the mother or primary caregiver has a desire for something other than simply the infant. Likewise, in a single parent family with a mother and child, the mere name of the absent father or even the mother's job can serve the function of S1. In a culture without fathers or husbands like the Na, a tribal totem can serve this function. Lacan's mathemes allow us to discern isomorphic functions served by contents that differ significantly from one another. With respect to the ontology presupposed by humanism, the mathemes allow us to discern a common structure behind a bewildering array of philosophical positions that differ from one another at the level of content, as well as common deadlocks that arise within these positions. As such, they allow us to more clearly orient our thinking in striving to overcome humanism.

2.
Lacan: Humanist and Posthumanist

Initially it might seem that Lacan and posthumanism make uncomfortable bedfellows. As Cary Wolfe has noted, Lacan remains squarely within the humanist tradition, in that he organizes his account of the subject around the opposition between the human and the animal.[10] Moreover, in *Encore* Lacan remarks that, "[t]he universe is the flower of rhetoric."[11] In making such an assertion, Lacan both repeats the gesture whereby being is subordinated to *logos* or the capacity for speech and rationality, and falls into what Quentin Meillassoux has called *correlationism*. As Meillassoux articulates it,

> Correlationism consists in disqualifying the claim that it is possible to consider the realms of subjectivity and objectivity independently of one another. Not only does it become necessary to insist that we never grasp an object

---

10 Cary Wolfe, *What is Posthumanism?*, pp. 39–47.
11 Jacques Lacan, *Encore: On Feminine Sexuality, The Limits of Love and Knowledge 1972–1973*, trans. Bruce Fink (New York, N.Y.: W.W. Norton & Company, 1998), p. 56.

"in itself", in isolation from its relation to the subject, but it also becomes necessary to maintain that we can never grasp a subject that would not always-already be related to an object.[12]

In this case, the correlationist gesture consists in the suture of the universe to language or rhetoric, such that the two can never be thought apart from one another. Indeed, as Lacan remarks fifteen years earlier, "[t]he real is without fissure,"[13] and he claims that "[t]here is no absence in the real."[14] It will thus be language, the symbolic, that brings differentiation and the play of presence and absence to the real, such that being can only ever be discussed in terms of what it is *for us*. As Stacy Alaimo says of such orientations of thought, "*[m]atter*, the vast stuff of the world and of ourselves, has been subdivided into manageable 'bits' or flattened into a 'blank slate' for human inscription."[15] As such, matter, the real, is seen as contributing nothing of its own and is treated as a passive and plastic medium, awaiting our inscription or differentiation. While Lacan professes an antihumanism in that he rejects the notion of a self-present and autonomous subject as a seat of agency and decision, he nonetheless remains within the humanist orbit in granting language this privileged place with respect to being. A genuinely posthumanist orientation must be capable of going beyond what things are *for us* and our language, so as to both think what they are *for themselves*, and what differences they contribute to assemblages.

Nonetheless, while Lacan is perpetually seduced by this humanist and correlationist tendency of thought, his discourse constantly exceeds itself, opening on to something beyond the human. As Bruce Fink puts it, Lacan's thought is "[...] a form of 'Gödelian structuralism,' [...] where every system is decompleted by the alterity or heterogeneity it contains within itself."[16] Fink overstates matters somewhat, because Lacan's thought is not merely a Gödelian structuralism, but also a Russellian structuralism. Over the course of his career, Lacan never ceases to explore the manner in which attempts to form totalities and wholes fail. These failures occur in two ways: A Gödelian way, or

12 Quentin Meillassoux, *After Finitude: An Essay on the Necessity of Contingency*, trans. Ray Brassier (New York, N.Y.: Continuum, 2008), p. 5.
13 Jacques Lacan, *Seminar II: The Ego in Freud's Theory and in the Technique of Psychoanalysis 1954–1955*, trans. Sylvana Tomaselli (New York, N.Y.: W.W. Norton & Company, 1988), p. 97.
14 Ibid., p. 313.
15 Alaimo, *Bodily Natures*, p. 1.
16 Bruce Fink, *The Lacanian Subject: Between Language and Jouissance* (Princeton, N.J.: Princeton University Press, 1995), p. xiv.

incompleteness, and a Russellian way, or inconsistency.[17] Attempts at totalization that generate incompleteness entail a constitutive exception that is undecidable within the system. Attempts at the formation of a whole that entail inconsistency show that every attempt to form a complete whole will be riddled with inconsistency. In short, every attempt to form a totality or whole encounters what Lacan refers to as the *Real* or "[…] an impasse of formalization."[18] These failures are of the utmost significance for posthumanist thought, for they show that every attempt to totalize being as a correlate of human thought, conceptuality, language, intentionality, or lived experience will encounter ruin from within, thereby pointing us to something beyond the human.

As Livingston demonstrates, every attempt to form a whole or totality runs afoul of either an incompleteness or an inconsistency.[19] The Gödelian failure necessarily generates a constitutive exception whose belonging to the system or truth or falsity within the system is undecidable. This would be the logic of sovereignty or the transcendent. Is the sovereign subject to the laws he institutes or not? Is God subject to the laws he institutes or not? Gödelian totalities institute a whole for all *other* beings, but only at the price of incompleteness or an exception whose relation to this system is undecidable. The Russellian failure necessarily generates an inconsistency when one attempts to form a totality. This is above all seen in the case of attempts to form a set of all sets that do not include *themselves*. Does the set of all sets that do not include themselves include itself or not? Does the Barber of Seville, who cuts everyone's hair except for those who cut their own hair, cut his own hair or does someone else cut his hair? If he cuts his own hair, then he has violated the stricture of cutting everyone's hair *except* those who cut their own hair. If he does not cut his own hair, then he has violated the requirement of cutting *everyone's* hair except those who cut their own hair. Such a totality is necessarily inconsistent. Totality is thus won at the price of incompleteness (in which case it is not a totality), or inconsistency (in which case it violates the strictures of logic).

In short, it is shown that totalities are impossible. With respect to posthumanism, this is of importance, for it demonstrates the impossibility of the human hegemonizing being through language, society,

---

17 For an excellent and well-informed account of the ethico-political importance of formalization and the manner in which the analytic and continental traditions have explored the implications of incompleteness and inconsistency, see also Paul Livingston, *The Politics of Logic: Badiou, Wittgenstein, and the Consequences of Formalism* (New York, N.Y.: Routledge, 2011).
18   Lacan, *Encore*, p. 93.
19   Compare Livingston, *The Politics of Logic*, chap. 1.

or culture. Here, then, the *Real* of Lacan's later thought is not the undifferentiated Real discussed earlier, nor is it the human reality that Lacan discusses as a synthesis of the imaginary and symbolic framed by fantasy,[20] but is rather a constitutive deadlock in formalization such that attempts to form totalities and wholes *necessarily* fail. These failures are of the utmost importance to both posthumanist thought and overcoming humanism, as they both inscribe the failure of the correlationist circle and point the way towards thinking an alterity and heterogeneity beyond the humanist subject, language, and culture.

I thus propose what Althusser called a *symptomatic reading* of Lacan's text. As Althusser puts it, "a reading [...] [that is] called '*symptomatic*' [...] divulges the undivulged event in the text it reads, and in the same movement relates it to *a different text*, present as a necessary absence in the first."[21] Like an analyst's listening to the speech of an analysand, such a reading aims not at the surface meaning and content of a text, but at those points where the text says more than it intends to say, where lacunae appear, where it slips and moves beyond itself. In Lacan it is as if there were two texts, a surface text and a shadow text, where the first is characterized by humanism in the form of claims of the sort that "the universe is the flower of rhetoric," while the second, through its explorations of the real or impasses of formalization, explodes the correlationist circle, providing passage beyond the human, language, and the correlationist circle. While I will not be able to fully develop such a project here, a Lacanian posthumanism would require us to carry out a thorough critique of his humanism, reworking his thought in terms of the real or those impasses of formalization that open us to a beyond of language and culture.

3.
The Graph of Sexuation: Two Ontologies

Although Lacan demonstrates the impossibility of forming totalities and wholes in a variety of ways, we find a particularly illuminating account of these impasses of formalization in Lacan's graph of sexuation presented in its completed form in *Encore*.[22]

---

20   Jacques Lacan, *The Four Fundamental Concepts of Psychoanalysis*, trans. Alan Sheridan (New York, N.Y.: W.W. Norton & Company, 1998), pp. 53–60.
21   Louis Althusser and Étienne Balibar, *Reading Capital*, trans. Ben Brewster (London: Verso, 2009), p. 29.
22   Lacan, *Encore*, p. 78.

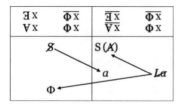

I will discuss the graph in more detail presently, but for the moment we need only note that the left-hand side is what Lacan defines as that of masculine sexuality, while the right is that of feminine sexuality. Here I will argue that the masculine side of Lacan's graph of sexuation presents us with the ontology of humanism, while the feminine side presents us with the ontology of posthumanism. Alternatively, we could say that the left-hand side presents us with ontologies of transcendence or sovereignty, while the right-hand side presents us with an ontology of immanence or a flat ontology. Finally, we can say that the masculine side is that of ontotheology, whereas the left is that of the crowned anarchy so beautifully explored by Deleuze. Wherever we have a masculine logic we also have a theology; even where that logic is atheistic in the more conventional sense of the term. For example, Laplace who famously responded to Napoleon's question of where God is in his system with the remark that he had no need of that hypothesis, nonetheless presents us with a theology insofar as he imagines the perspective of a sovereign subject that knows the position and velocity of each particle in the universe. That is, he imagines an exception that is outside of and above the system it surveys.

Lacan's graph of sexuation presents us with two fundamentally different ontologies of the world. If this thesis holds up, it will be seen that there is also a deep complicity between humanism, patriarchy, and ontotheology (all of these configurations will be seen to be structurally isomorphic and are forms of transcendence or sovereignty) as well as a deep connection between posthumanism and feminism. Where femininity has, throughout the philosophical tradition, been presented as the side of semblance or masquerade—of untruth—I argue instead that it is the side of masculinity that is the side of semblance, masquerade, or ontological untruth. In other words, I will argue that the ontology presented on the masculine side of the graph of sexuation is a fundamental distortion of the being of being. This will require showing that on the feminine side we get an immanent genesis of masculine structure or that masculine structure is, in fact, built on feminine structure.

However, before proceeding, it is necessary to discuss the relationship between the graph of sexuation and biological sex and gender. In this connection, Bruce Fink reminds us that,

> It should be recalled that sexuation is not biological sex: What Lacan calls masculine structure and feminine structure have to do not with one's biological organs but rather with the kind of jouissance one is able to obtain. There is not, to the best of my knowledge, any easy overlap between sexuation and "gender," between sexuation and "sexual identity," or between sexuation and what is sometimes referred to as "sexual orientation."[23]

In other words, a person can occupy either the masculine or feminine side of the graph of sexuation regardless of gender, biological sex, or sexual orientation. Insofar as the graph has a tenuous relation to biological sex, I propose to read them as articulating the basic structure of two different ontologies, rather than as discussions of sexuation. As Slavoj Žižek writes,

> There is a link between ontological and sexual difference (conceived in a purely formal-transcendental way, along the lines of Lacan's "formulas of sexuation," of course). The male side—universality and exception—is literally "meta-physical" (the entire universe, all of reality, is grounded in its constitutive exception, the highest entity which is *epkeina tes ousias*), while the ontological difference proper is feminine: reality is non-all, but there is nothing beyond-outside it, and this Nothing is Being itself.[24]

While I do not follow Žižek in his Hegelian development of these two ontologies, I do believe he gets the basic difference in ontologies right. Insofar as the masculine side of the graph of sexuation is articulated around a constitutive exception, it forms a *meta-physic* in the Heideggerian sense of ontotheology and is organized around a logic of the transcendent and sovereignty. Here, the sovereign or transcendent is that which grounds all of being, without itself being subject to the law that it institutes and without being dependent on anything else. Like a self-similar and repeating fractal pattern, we thus see that there is an isomorphism between the God of theistic religions, kings with respect

---

23   Bruce Fink, *Lacan to the Letter: Reading Écrits Closely* (Minneapolis, Minn.: University of Minnesota Press, 2004), p. 158. Due to limitations of space, I here omit discussion of how the graph of sexuation articulates the two ways in which jouissance can fail. For a detailed discussion of this, compare Levi R. Bryant, *The Democracy of Objects* (Ann Arbor, Mich.: Open Humanities Press, 2011), section 6.1.
24   Slavoj Žižek, *The Parallax View* (Cambridge, Mass.: The MIT Press, 2006), p. 24.

to their subjects, Platonic forms (and above all the *form* of the Good discussed in *The Republic*), the God of negative theology, the father as understood in Oedipus, CEOs, and so forth. Insofar as the human is treated as a constitutive and unique exception to all other beings, humanism too would obey this logic. By contrast, the feminine side of the graph of sexuation bars any constitutive exception, treating being as a flat plane without any genuine sovereigns or transcendent beings. In this way, it identifies a posthuman ontology insofar as humans are no longer conceived as lords or sovereigns of being, but as beings among beings.

4.
Masculine Ontology: Humanist Logics of Exception

Bruce Fink's observation that both biological males and females can occupy either side of the graph makes it something of a mystery as to why Lacan refers to these sides as masculine or feminine at all. As far as I have been able to discern, Lacan associates the left side of the graph with masculinity because it presents us with a highly abstract and formalized depiction of the Oedipus complex written as follows:

$$\exists x \sim \Phi x$$
$$\forall x \; \Phi x$$

In second-order symbolic logic, the symbol "$\exists$" is known as an *existential quantifier* and is read *there exists a...* For example, the proposition *The cat is on the mat* would be written "$(\exists x)(Cx \; \& \; Mx)$," which would read *there exists an entity such that that entity is a cat and that entity is on a mat*. The symbol "$\forall$" is known as a *universal quantifier* and is read *all*. Thus, the proposition *all cats are felines* would be written $(\forall x)(Cx \rightarrow Fx)$, which would be read *for all entities x, if x is a cat, then x is a feline*. The symbol "$\sim$" is the sign for negation. And finally, Lacan introduces the symbol "Φ" to designate the phallic function, the incest prohibition, the law, castration, or limitation. Within a Lacanian framework, "Φ" does not refer to the penis but to the manner in which lack is introduced into the world by language.

We are now in a position to read the two propositions of the masculine side of Lacan's graph of sexuation. The first or upper proposition, $\exists x \sim \Phi x$, reads *there exists an entity such that this entity is not subject to the phallic function*. The lower proposition, $\forall x \; \Phi x$, reads *for all entities, those entities are subject to the phallic function*. We are now in a position to see why Lacan associates these two propositions with masculinity. What we have here is the Oedipal structure where one being—the being articulated in the upper proposition—refers to the father that lays down the law or prohibition of incest while not himself being prohibited by that restriction (he is able to enjoy his partner), while the lower proposition articulates all of those beings subject to this law or restriction. Alternatively, we have here a formalization of Freud's myth of the primal father articulated in *Totem and Taboo*, where the primal father has no restrictions on his enjoyment insofar as he is able to enjoy *all* women—including his own mother, his sisters, and his daughters—while all of the other men in the tribe are prohibited from enjoying *any* women in the tribe.

Both the myth of the primal father and the Oedipus are, of course, patriarchal or masculine structures. Why, then, does Lacan not simply say that he is speaking about the Oedipus and the myth of the primal father? Well first, as we saw earlier, it is not necessary for a biological male to actually be present for this structure to be instantiated (a woman can serve the function of lawgiver in a lesbian relationship), nor for a second man or woman to even be present for this structure to function (the *name-of-the-father* can do the job in, for example, the case of a totem or a single parent family of its own accord). However, second, and more importantly, this formalization allows us to discern a wide variety of patriarchal structures where we might otherwise think these structures have nothing to do with patriarchy whatsoever. Insofar as the patriarch, $\exists x \sim \Phi x$, is treated as an origin of the law and an exception to the law, there is a structural isomorphism between the Oedipus and the myth of the primal father and the God of theistic or monotheistic religions, sovereigns, corporate CEOs, Platonic forms, ahistorical essences, dictators, charismatic leaders, and so on and so forth. This would also include the *humanist subject*, where the human is treated as that which is sovereign over nature and as free from the *animal* limitations of embodiment, materiality, and embeddedness through its exceptional capacity for reason. What we discover is a structural isomorphy between ontotheology or metaphysics—those ontological orientations that discern being as arising out of a single ground or origin—and patriarchy, and humanism.

The important thing to note about the masculine side of the graph of sexuation is that it is not possible for *both* propositions to be true. It cannot simultaneously be the case that *all* beings are subject to the phallic function, castration, or limitation, and for there to exist *an* entity that is not subject to this function. As a consequence, structures organized around this sort of transcendence will necessarily be fraught by paradox from within. It is at the lower level of the graph—what might be called *the cell of jouissance*—that we encounter the consequences of this paradoxical and unstable structure. There, it is as if the structure of the upper level marks its own impossibility. Here we see $, the sign for the barred subject, pointing to a, the *objet a*. Here we can read the barred subject ($) in one of two ways: Either we can read the barred subject as the correlate of the proposition $\forall x \; \Phi x$, where the castration or sacrifice the subject undergoes in existing necessarily entails a divided or split subject that has lost something. Here, then, the fact that all beings necessarily sacrifice jouissance in order to exist entails the formation of a *fantasy*—$\exists x \sim \Phi x$—or the belief in the existence of a being that is not castrated or limited. This fantasy, in turn, generates the experience of ourselves as necessarily split. Or, we can read the barred subject as the correlate of the very impossibility of this structure itself; a structure in which it is simultaneously held that *all* beings are subject to the phallic function and where there exists an exception to the phallic function.

Insofar as this structure insists that *both* propositions are true despite the fact that they stand in stark contradiction to one another, the impossibility of the structure, the real, comes to be encountered as an *accident*, rather than as a necessary and ineluctable feature of this structure. This accident is marked by the *objet a*, which Lacan describes variously as a remainder, excess, and surplus that evades symbolization. As an accident, the *objet a* is not seen as a *necessary* and ineluctable consequence of this structure but as a contingent *glitch*, an imperfection, that can be surmounted through either the eradication of the *objet a*, or through the uniting of the barred subject and the *objet a*. This is why we see a variation of Lacan's formula for obsessional fantasy[25]—$ < > a—in the lower portion of the masculine side of the graph of sexuation. The fantasy here is that which strives to cover over the constitutive incompleteness of this structure. This covering over can be carried out in a variety of ways. In *Seminar 10*, Lacan suggests that we read the *punch* of the formulas of fantasy— $ < > $ —as articulating the logical function of conjunction (&) and disjunction (v), or the arithmetical functions of *greater than* (>) or *less than* (<). Obsessional, masculine fantasy could thus take four forms: ($ & a), ($ v a), ($ > a), or ($ < a). In the first form, we would have the barred subject conjoined with the element that is missing so as to surmount the incompleteness of the symbolic order. For example, this could be the humanist fantasy of surmounting nature through technology, or the consumerist fantasy of completing oneself through the

---

25   As Bruce Fink observes, the formula for obsessional fantasy is written ($ < > a), whereas the formula for fantasy in hysteria is written (a < > -A-). Compare Bruce Fink, *A Clinical Introduction to Lacanian Psychoanalysis*, pp. 258–259.

acquisition of goods, or the idea of a historical dialectic eventually perfecting man. In the second form, disjunction, we get an either/or that would be at the foundation of various racisms, sexisms, religious fundamentalisms, and nationalisms. Here the racial other is seen as that remainder, that accident, that prevents the social order from achieving totality and completeness and the fantasy consists in the belief that if that other were simply eradicated, social disharmony would finally be surmounted. In the third form of fantasy, the domination of other beings or groups is seen as the condition for finally achieving totality and social harmony; while finally in the fourth form, complete submission to some authority or divinity is seen as the condition for achieving social completeness and harmony.[26]

The key point is that within logics of exception, masculinity, or sovereignty, this fantasy structure is an *ineluctable* and *necessary* consequence of the structure but is seen by those as occupying the structure as an accidental state of affairs that could possibly be overcome if we simply attended to the *object a* or remainder in the appropriate way.[27] Logics of exception or sovereignty will *necessarily* generate racisms, ethnocentrisms, sexisms, forms of domination, and forms of exploitation as a consequence of the relationship between their constitutive incompleteness and the structure of fantasy that supplements them and allows them to function despite their impossibility. In the case of humanism, where the human is treated as a sovereign exception to the rest of being, it would thus be no accident that humanism has been accompanied by colonial violence, exploitation of the world, and nationalistic violence.[28]

---

26 For a detailed discussion of how the masculine ontologies systematically generate persecution of an other, see also Levi R. Bryant, "The Other Face of God: Lacan, Theological Structure, and the Accursed Remainder," in: *Speculations III* (Brooklyn, N.Y.: punctum books, 2016).
27 It is precisely this ineluctable relation that Agamben outlines in the relation between sovereignty and bare life. Compare Giorgio Agamben, *Homo Sacer: Sovereign Power and Bare Life*, trans. Daniel Heller-Roazen (Redwood City, Calif.: Stanford University Press, 1998). My claim is that this structure appears not only in those political orders organized around sovereignty, but are to be found in any ontology organized around masculinity or the logic of exception.
28 Here we find a profound affinity between Adorno's analysis of the relationship between violence and ontology in Theodor W. Adorno, *Negative Dialectics*, trans. E.B. Ashton, (New York, N.Y.: Continuum, 1973), and Lacan's analysis of masculine sexuation. The difference would be that whereas Adorno seems to hold that violence is an ineluctable consequence of ontology *as such*, Lacan sees it as a feature of ontologies structured in terms of the masculine; opening the possibility of ontologies that do not issue in this outcome.

This sheds light on an enigmatic claim Lacan makes in *Encore* that all men are *hommesexual*.[29] Lacan is not making the claim that all men are sexually oriented towards other men, but rather that masculine sexuality/ontology is oriented towards a logic of sameness and identity. It is a digestive logic that says to all alterity, *you will be assimilated*. Moreover, it is premised on the erasure of alterity altogether. In this connection, it is important to recognize Lacan's pun on *homosexuality*, drawing on the word *homme*, signifying, in French, *man*. For the masculine logic of jouissance and desire, we get a logic of domestication, where alterity and difference must either be eradicated or metabolized in terms of the masculine self-image. The masculine formula for fantasy—$ < > a$—says nothing more than this. This is why masculine sexuation systematically leads to a logic of domination, obedience, exploitation, and violence. Moreover, here it can be seen that the very core of correlationism is *hommesexual* in its foreclosure of the possibility of thinking being and thought apart from one another. It necessarily reduces the world to the alienated reflection of man.

5.
Feminine Ontology: Logics of Posthuman Immanence

On the feminine side of the graph of sexuation, we encounter a very different ontology; an ontology without exception or sovereignty. Lacan inscribes feminine sexuation as follows:

$$\sim \exists x \sim \Phi x$$
$$\sim \forall x \; \Phi x$$

Here the upper proposition reads, *there does not exist an entity that is not subject to the phallic function*. By contrast, the lower proposition reads, *not all of any entity is subject to the phallic function*.[30] The first point to note about this second ontology is that it is *without exception*. Here *every* being that exists is subject to the phallic function, castration, or limitation, such that if there is a God or there are sovereigns, these beings are not *exceptions* but are themselves mediated in exactly the same way as any other being. For example, as Hegel observes in his

---

29 Lacan, *Encore*, p. 84.

30 In *Encore*, Bruce Fink translates the logical function "$\forall$" as *whole*. I have instead opted to translate it as *all* because 1) the term *whole* is never used in symbolic logic, and 2) the translation of "$\forall$" as *whole* carries the suggestion that women are lacking or incomplete in some way.

account of the master/servant dialectic, the king is only a king because his *servants* recognize him as a king.[31] His power does not arise from special and enigmatic feature of his being but rather from the manner in which he is socially recognized. The king is not transcendent to his subjects but is among his subjects, albeit in a disguised way. The same would hold true of God. As a consequence, this second ontology places all beings on a "flat plane" without sovereigns or transcendent terms. As a consequence, humans are no longer privileged or sovereign terms within being but are beings *among* other beings.

Second, where the two propositions on the masculine side of the graph of sexuation stand in contradiction to one another such that they *both* cannot be true, the same is not true with the propositions on the feminine side of the graph of sexuation. The propositions *there does not exist an entity that is not subject to the phallic function* and *not all of any entity is subject to the phallic function* are neither contraries nor contradictories of one another. Rather, the first articulates the claim that there are no sovereigns transcendent or otherwise, that there is no entity not subject to limitation (that is, only finite entities exist), while the second claims that, nonetheless, there is something of every entity that evades or escapes subordination to other entities. In other words, this would be the claim that no entity can be *reduced* to what it is—whether through perception, conceptuality, language, culture, power, and so forth—for another entity. There is always something that escapes or evades subordination. There is thus a deep ontological difference between the masculine side's claim that *all entities are subject to the phallic function* which supposes that beings can be exhausted in their subordination—for example, that language could exhaust the world—and the claim that *not all of any entity is subject to the phallic function*. The latter asserts that there is always something that eludes subordination.

Lacan generally associates the phallic function with our alienation in language. Castration (the phallic function) refers not to the fear that men will have their penises cut off, but rather to the manner in which we must pursue our jouissance through the detour of language, the law, or the symbolic, and also to the way we are identified or defined by language. For example, even if a child is adopted, the incest prohibition still holds because familial identity is a *symbolic* function defined by a signifying position within the symbolic order, not a biological function. We are alienated in our symbolic identities and reduced to them. However, in claiming that the feminine side is *not-all*, that there

31 G.W.F. Hegel, *Hegel's Phenomenology of Spirit*, trans. A.V. Miller (Oxford: Oxford University Press, 1977), pp. 111–117.

is something that eludes and evades the phallic function, Lacan marks the opening to the posthuman. For where no being can be reduced to a correlate for human thought, language, culture, society, power, and so forth, it follows that space is opened for the nonhuman or that which is beyond the human.

Here we can theorize this *not-all* in terms of Lacan's controversial *feminine jouissance*. Lacan argued that feminine sexuation is such that *women* are capable of a non-phallic jouissance outside the symbolic order. Where masculine jouissance is necessarily phallic, and where phallic jouissance is a jouissance that finds enjoyment in the symbolic order—titles, professional accomplishments, prestige, wealth, and so forth—that dreams of a final ground or master-term that would halt all play of the signifier and that operates according to a logic of identity and sameness where subject and object would surmount all alterity, feminine jouissance opens on to an enjoyment outside the symbolic and cultural that does not seek an ultimate ground and that is capable of relating to alterity *qua* alterity. For example, rather than treating the animal as *poor in world*, as Heidegger does in *The Fundamental Concepts of Metaphysics*,[32] thereby subordinating the animal to the measure of man or the human, a feminine framework would approach the animal in terms of what it is, rather than what it is not. In a feminine ontology, beings are not measured in terms of a transcendent term but in terms of what they are for themselves. In this regard, they are no longer reduced to the linguistic.

Here we encounter the significance of Lacan's notorious claim that *la femme n'existe pas* (the Woman does not exist).[33] Lacan, of course, holds that *women* exist, but denies that there is an essence that could define the essence common to *all* woman giving rise to the form *Woman*. If this is so, then it is because *not all of woman is subject to language or the phallic function*, $\sim \forall x \; \Phi x$; there is always something that escapes, within this ontology, linguistic identification and reduction. As a consequence, women are the true singularities. They are irreducible to *types* or linguistic *kinds*. Where masculine sexuation or ontology is defined by *hommesexuality* or a logic of the same and identity, feminine ontology is characterized by a logic of alterity or difference. It relates to the other *as* other, rather than as a blank screen awaiting human inscription to become a mirror of ourselves. It is in this regard that feminine ontology is posthuman, for it neither practices

---

32 Martin Heidegger, *The Fundamental Concepts of Metaphysics: World, Finitude, Solitude*, trans. William McNeill and Nicholas Walker (Bloomington, Ind.: Indiana University Press, 2001).

33 Lacan, *Encore*, p. 7.

human exceptionalism, nor treats alterity as an alterity to be domesticated or metabolized by human language, culture, or intentionality. Insofar as we have resolved to read the graph ontologically, there is no reason to restrict this non-existence to Woman, but rather we can extend this non-existence of types, kinds, or essences to *all* beings. There is no being that can be reduced to the correlate of human conceptuality, language, or intentionality.

This point is above all marked in the lower cell of the feminine side of the graph of sexuation where we see the non-existent Woman (-*La*-) pointing to S(-A-). "S(-A-)" denotes *the signifier of the barred Other*. Lacan associates the Other with the symbolic order or language (S2). In the "Rome Discourse," he remarks that "the symbol first manifests itself as the killing of the thing."[34] The signifier kills the thing in three ways: First, it introduces absence into the world. Once something is named, it is possible to refer to it in its absence. Indeed, it is possible to refer to entities that do not exist at all. Second, the symbol reifies the thing, turning it into a fixed identity or nature, despite the fact that all things change and become. Finally, it kills the thing by reducing the singular, the irreplaceable, to the equivalent according to a linguistic type. The signifier, as it were, replaces the thing and erases its singularity. In being directed towards the *barred* Other, it is precisely this erasure that is refused in feminine ontology. Where masculine ontology reduces the things of the world—human and nonhuman—to a positionality within the symbolic order, feminine ontology relates to things in their irreplaceable singularity. Above all, things are not reduced to being a correlate for human language, culture, intentionality, power, discourse, and so forth. In this regard, where masculine ontology is characterized by hommesexuality, feminine sexuation is characterized by heterosexuality. Here *heterosexuality* does not signify orientations towards the opposite sex, but rather orientation towards *irreducible alterity*. It is that orientation that refuses reduction of others and nonhumans to the symbol.

6.

Masculine Masquerade

Should there be a question of *choosing* one of these ontologies over the other? We should recall that an ontology is not *being* itself, but rather

---

34 Jacques Lacan, "The Function and Field of Speech and Language in Psychoanalysis," in *Écrits*, trans. Bruce Fink (New York, N.Y.: W.W. Norton & Co., 2006), p. 262.

a *theory of being*. Is there, then, any reason for preferring one ontology over the other? We have seen, of course, that there are all sorts of ethico-political reasons for preferring feminine ontology over masculine ontology. Masculine ontology seems to lead to a logic of submission, exploitation, violence, and assimilation, whereas feminine ontology is open to alterity and difference. However, as compelling as these arguments are in an ethico-political arena, such reasoning would be a violation of the is/ought distinction, allowing our beliefs about what ought to be the case to dictate what *is* the case. However, just because one believes that nuclear weapons ought not exist, it does not follow that they do not exist. It could just be that being itself is organized around a logic of sovereignty.

If we are to argue that being as such is a feminine structure, we need specifically *ontological* reasons for such a claim. In this connection, the first point to note is that the masculine theory of being is *contradictory*. Insofar as a contradiction cannot be true, it follows that this theory of being cannot be true. Yet if masculine structure is false and feminine ontology is true, why is it that it has been the dominant theory of being throughout the history of philosophy? What is it that accounts for the persistent masquerade and illusion of sovereignty, completeness, humanism, and transcendence throughout the history of philosophy?

The lower portion of the graph of sexuation suggests an answer; for there we see an arrow pointing not only to the barred or non-existent Other—S(-A-)—but to Φ as well. Here "Φ" signifies something different from what it does in the upper portions of the graph. In the upper portions of the graph Φ signifies limitation, castration, incompleteness, and sacrifice. By contrast, in the lower portion of the graph it signifies potency or completeness. Here Φ can function in one of two ways in the economy of desire and jouissance: On the one hand, a person can *identify* with a phallic figure as a subject that possesses (imagined) potency and completeness as in the case of a scholar, an all-knowing God, scientist, wealthy person, celebrity, physically strong person, and so on. The subject looks to an other imagined as complete and capable of naming non-existent Woman within the symbolic order; the subject, -La-, would look to an *other* capable of sustaining their being and identity. On the other hand, desire and jouissance oriented towards Φ can signify a subject that strives to *cover over* and *erase* the incompleteness and limitation at the heart of feminine ontological structure through coming to embody wealth, power, knowledge, strength, and so on. In short, within the feminine ontological framework we get the genesis of the masculine fantasy, $\exists x \sim \Phi x$, characteristic of masculine ontology.

47

Note in this context that where femininity goes unmarked within masculine structure, masculine structure is marked as one of the possibilities of thought and subjectivization within feminine structure. Put differently, it is as if there is always a tendency within immanence to erase immanence and erect a transcendence that would overcome incompleteness and limitation. Immanence, as it were, generates its own *transcendental illusion* that covers over the truth of immanence. Speaking in the context of Kant's account of transcendental illusions, Deleuze remarks that Kant "substituted [the concept of transcendental] illusion [for that of error]: internal illusions, interior to reason, instead of errors from without which were merely effects of bodily causes."[35] Elsewhere, Deleuze remarks that "[t]he illusions are said to be inevitable and even to result from the nature of reason [...]. All Critique can do is to exorcise the effects of illusion on knowledge itself, but it cannot prevent its formation in the faculty of knowledge."[36] Where a simple error is a failed adequation between a proposition about the world and the world itself, a transcendental illusion is an illusion that arises from within thought itself.

What I claim is that masculine ontology is a transcendental illusion of this sort. If this is true, then two consequences would follow: First, there would *not* be *two* irreducible ontologies—the masculine and the feminine—such that the decision between the two of them cannot be made, but rather there is only one ontology—feminine ontology—that *generates* the transcendental illusion of masculine ontology within it. Second, it would turn out that masculinity is *masquerade* insofar as it strives to erase and cover over the constitutive finitude of being through the erection of a transcendent, unlimited term.

Can evidence within Lacanian theory be marshaled in support of this hypothesis? Due to limitations of space, my argument here must be impressionistic.[37] In *The Sublime Object of Ideology*, Žižek notes that "the subject as such is hysterical."[38] If the subject is, at its core, hysterical, then this is because subject names precisely that which cannot be placed or named within the symbolic order. However, that which

35 Gilles Deleuze, *Difference and Repetition*, trans. Paul Patton (New York, N.Y.: Columbia University Press, 1994), p. 136.
36 Gilles Deleuze, *Kant's Critical Philosophy*, trans. Hugh Tomlinson and Barbara Habberjam (Minneapolis, Minn.: University of Minnesota Press, 1984), p. 25.
37 For a detailed discussion of how masculinity is masquerade, see also Levi R. Bryant, *The Democracy of Objects* (Ann Arbor, Mich.: Open Humanities Press, 2011), section 6.1.
38 Slavoj Žižek, *The Sublime Object of Ideology* (London: Verso Books, 1997), p. 181.

cannot be named within the symbolic order is structurally isomorphic to Lacan's thesis that *la femme n'existe pas*. That is, subject and femininity are structurally synonymous with one another. Indeed, psychoanalysis has long associated hysteria with femininity. This claim is radical because it asserts that all subjects, whether biologically male or female, are at root structurally feminine. However, this is not all. Žižek goes on to remark that

> hysteria and obsessional neurosis are not two species of neurosis as a neutral-universal genus; their relation is a dialectical one—it was Freud himself who noted that obsessional neurosis is a kind of 'dialectic of hysteria' hysteria as a fundamental determination of a neurotic position contains two species, obsessional neurosis *and itself as its own species*.[39]

Obsessional neurosis is, of course, associated with masculinity. Yet if obsessional neurosis is a subspecies of hysteria, it follows that hysteria, the feminine, is the *ontological root* of masculine ontology. Both masculine ontology and subjectivity would thus be a sort of *recoil*, a repression, of feminine immanence and finitude. It would be a form of thought that strives to both cover over the ontological truth of immanence, while also ineluctably carrying the trace of finitude and immanence.

Despite Lacan's own tendency towards *anti-humanist humanism*, we find the resources for both thinking beyond the human and human exceptionalism through the careful disclosure of the limits of language and culture and the paradoxes that haunt attempts to totalize being in humanistic terms through masculine ontologies and the possibility of a critique of the transcendental illusions characteristic of masculine ontology. Lacan's posthumanism—a posthumanism that he never articulated himself, but that becomes available with his final work—calls for us to dismantle both masculine ontology and the way it functions in epistemological, ethical, and political thought. It also calls for a project of attending to beings as their own measure of themselves, opening ourselves to alterity *qua* alterity and a project of refusing the treatment of beings as alienated reflections of human conceptuality, language, and intentionality.

---

39 Ibid., p. 191.

Arantzazu Saratxaga Arregi

Girl: A Paradigmatic Example of
Evolutionary Disobedience

1.
The Girl (das Mädchen):
An Excluded Third in the Framework of Anthropogeneric Bivalences

*a) The framework of anthropogeneric relations: analyzing phallic
univalence (1) and its isomorphic complementary (0) propaedeutically*

Consider the German term for the girl, *das Mädchen*. It is neither feminine nor masculine; it is grammatically neutral. The article that defines the generic difference of the girl escapes a bivalent logic (0/1): The girl is neutral. It is neither masculine (1) nor its negation, feminine (0). Thus, the gender relationship between male and female is less a relationship characterized by difference, but rather one of complementarity and isomorphic correspondence.

At this point, we have to square up to the tradition and discipline of psychoanalysis, which is responsible for subsuming the anthropological and libidinal semantic into a logical structure of two values: an affirmative proposition of unique universal absolute value (1/+) and its negation (0/−).

According to the psychoanalytic tradition shared by Freud and Lacan, the function of the term *phallus*, both in the sense of genitalia (Freud) and in its dimension of a symbolic signifier (Lacan), represents the value *of the truth, which asserts itself*. It is identical with itself and refers to itself. Psychoanalysis has defined the framework of anthropogeneric relations according to this bivalent logical relation, which rests on the assertion of a unique universal type, that is to say it provides a unique signifier and universal value to the *phallus*. This affirmation is absolute: The phallus is (1). The denial of the predicate falls into the order of reflection (0), and thus the feminine *is not*. Between man and his denial, the feminine as a third *is excluded* (tertium non datur). This logic determines our way of thinking and the structuring of our gender relations. The feminine represents the complementary masculine (0/−) and, in this case, the absence of the phallus.

Masculine and *feminine* form a relationship of contrariety and therefore also of isomorphic complementariness. When it comes to human beings, gender is bivalent: *either* masculine (1) or feminine (0) and given the logical impossibility of being one *and* the other simultaneously, both cannot be true because they differ in quality and therefore form a relationship of complementary symmetry. This note about the relationship of contrariety between the universal male gender and the universal female gender serves as an explanatory note to a detail which, in the majority of cases, goes unnoticed: the oppositional relation of male/female is a qualitative difference because it is commonly universal; the two maintain a relationship of complementary symmetry. The Woman(-Human Genus) differentiates herself from the Man(-Human Genus), while both belong to the same universal genus (human). Therefore, the neutral determines a genre that is neither male nor female; it escapes a bivalent logic and falls into the excluded third (tertium non datur).

The penis retains univalent and absolute values (1), whereas the woman is its opposite (0). A third value is excluded in the difference of *penis* and so-called *penis envy*, namely *the girl* (n).

The girl's potential refers to the point where she indicates an excluded third according to the Freudian psychoanalytic framework. I take the Freudian doctrine as a starting point because its subdivision in *female versus male* is based on the *univalence of the phallus*, which emphasizes the metaphysical doctrine of identity. It therefore conforms with the anthropogeneric being of the girl, the blind spot of the bivalent gender construct, and allows us to consider the anthropogenerically paradoxical classification of the girl.

b) Freudian derivations:
a body which houses a matrix in latency is an excluded third

According to the etymology of these notions and their meaning, one could say that *das Mädchen*, originally meaning the *little* maid, *little* Virgin or *little* single woman, exposes the failure of the realization of an attribute assigned to the female body, the potential of reproduction. Thus, the neuter (n) retains the meaning of the non-realization of the negative complement (0/–) of the masculine value (1/+). Through the evolution of language, the explicit semantic value of the diminutive suffix (*-chen*) was lost. Nevertheless, it retained the quality of not bringing the potential of reproduction to fruition in order to designate the specific difference of a group of elements whose genital functionality has not yet been attained.

The diachronic evolution of the term girl finds that the semiotization of the girl's body—for purely biological reasons—endorses once more the existence of a unique genus that affirms itself: man. The woman becomes its complement, and the girl is, according to the traditional sense of its meaning, a *not-yet* being. As we see, its definition is based on biological reasoning. The girl is the miniature version of the woman who has not yet complied with its specific difference: reproduction. Such a biological argument, however, serves as a propaedeutic exercise for further analysis in the field of semantics, i.e. its language and its symbols, as well as what societies do with a body in a state of becoming, and also what the relationship of the excluded third would be with respect to the uterine filiation (girl/the woman/mothers).

The generalization of the ability to procreate identifies the special somatic characteristic of the girl, whose logical expression aligns paradoxically to identity metaphysics (excluded thirds) and whose taxonomy indicates a third category. In this sense, the special position of the girl is not based on biological determinism but on a gender codification that goes back to the ontomorphogenetic event (that contains a living environment or matrix) in a state of latency. The body of the girl phenomenologically determines a speculative matrixial space which has not yet been realized in the world.

b.1) Body of the girl:
the realism of a body without organs

The girl designates a third party, excluded from a social order only insofar as her body houses a *matrix* in a *state of potentiality*. This *body without an organ* is a real signifier that defies the dual structure on which the genital organization of the human being, its introduction into the social body, and its libidinal economy rests.

The *realism* of the body of the girl is less a naturalist objectivism than a *speculative assignment* of value in a state of latency and becoming. Far from approaching a biologistic position, it is suitable to understand the body of the girl in the framework of a speculative symbolism, which transforms it into social structures. Therefore, the latter impose a form of realism onto the body of the girl via anthropogeneric structures, which result in a body characterized by the maintenance of the latent state of an organ that produces life. This potentiality threatens the bivalent structure 1/0.

Following this psychoanalytical framework, the girl opens a channel to critical reflection on the *filial uterine structure*. Mother, woman, and girl: all of them have potential. However, such potentiality serves a libidinal economy, which regulates mother, woman, and girl and is then projected on social order as the symbolic figure that will determine the specific differences between mother, woman, and girl.

The purpose of linking the girl with the uterine filial chain is to consider the paradoxical position of the girl—tertium non datur—with the generic value of 0, or the feminine. The Freudian framework serves to question the nature of the anthropogeneric relationships—to put it differently: *How female is the girl?*

The grammatical neuter gender places the girl on the edge of logical associations, and this figure leads to a deployment of the symbolic hermeneutics of the *excluded third*. It is neither $(1/+)$, nor is it identified as its opposite $(0/-)$, except in a relative way. The figure of the girl is identified in a relative way with the group of mothers, because both groups stay in the same body, the difference being their respective potential for realization. The girl so far is positioned between $(1/+)$ and its denial, i.e. $(0/-)$.

Therefore, talking about the figure of the girl means defining the boundaries of socialization by which an individual will leave a particular group (girls) in order to integrate into another (women) through a medium (mothers). Hence, the girl is a key figure in the formation of social groups. *This*, the girl, is a key element in shaping the social fabric. *It* will be fundamental to the design and regulation of social contours. *It* will assume a central role in the inclusive/exclusive regulation of a group (only that which reinforces and intensifies the exclusivity of the group is worthy of being included in it). *It*, the girl, is the technical device in the self-generation of boundaries.

For this reason, a study of the girl sheds light on the fringes of the structural machine of culture, and takes its judgments and tautologies to its limits. *It* leads us to unmask the ineffable mysteries of the unknown continent of psychoanalysis, since it is *it* that marks the limit of the theorems of castration and their oedipal axioms. *It* alone enables us to consider the development of *the woman* as a phenomenon existing only in the context of the oedipal *polis*. *It* alone allows us to make remarks about an *artificial gender*, which is why the recent theoretical interest in the figure of the girl is not surprising. The girl, in its logically aporetic nature, elicits questions regarding the structure of modern societies from an interdisciplinary perspective.

This study's aim is to explain the type of relationship that exists between girls, mothers, and women in order to define a genesis derived from *uterine descent*. In order to accomplish this, it is necessary to find an answer to the question: What is the link between a third, excluded party (n) and the phallic univalence $(1/+)$, which has determined the oedipal libidinal structure of modern societies? What is the relationship of the girl (n) to the isomorphic supplement (0/–) of the male libido? This leads us to analyze the semiotic figure of the girl formally within the framework of a *uterine trilogy* (girl–the woman–mothers) structured by the productivity the uterus as well as its role in the economic organization of a social body. The girl also requires two critical perspectives: On the one hand, the locality of the girl in the context of a culture that repeats the circulation of stolen bodies (i.e. slavery), rape, sex and broken bonds, and, on the other, the assessment of the generic autonomy of the girl (n) as a logical stage that aims to develop an artificial gender.

The girl designates the existence of *matrixial* space that has not yet revealed itself. It exists in latency and symbolizes the maintenance of a living space for the ontogenetic development (uterus), which is nevertheless marked by the potential allocation for reproducibility. The girl is distinctive of a *speculative* matrixiality because she contains a not-yet-activated functionality that has been allocated a living environment (uterus).

2.
A Theorem for *the Woman* that Does Not Exist

Numerous studies attribute an inversely proportional value to the girl as well as to the boy, as if the boy's sexual development was symmetrical to an arena of uterine infantilization. The girl harbors an organ of pure potential. The question of how and when a girl becomes a woman has to be answered by taking into account the conditions under which the girl is presented as a negative and/or complementary sign for the boy.

At this point, I shall call into question a matter some researchers and scholars who have engaged in the study of the girl have deemed all-too-obvious.[1] Their claim that the girl is the negative complement of the boy is based on the assumption that the girl is a little woman, and therefore incomplete. That the girl contains a matrix in a state of pure potentiality means that this matrix takes part in the invisible nature of creation.[2] Its state of latency, however, is so powerful that it becomes

---

1 Compare Helga Kelle, "Mädchen: Zur Entwicklung der Mädchenforschung," in *Handbuch Frauen- und Geschlechterforschung: Theorie, Methoden, Empirie*, ed. Ruth Becker, Beate Kortendiek (Wiesbaden: Springer, 2010).

2 Compare Lucien Braun, "L'idée de 'Matrix' chez Paracelse," in *Paracelsus und seine internationale Rezeption in der frühen Neuzeit. Beiträge zur Geschichte des Paracelsus*, ed. Heinz Schott and Iliana Zinger, (Leiden: Brill, 1998), p. 17.

a value of exchange that carries a speculative value on the price of life. This value will be projected onto a system of laws and prohibitions that determine the circulation of goods in a group and will be the agent of her integration into the body of culture, which encodes the value of the body without organs of the girl. The *becoming-girl* acquires a categorical value in the symbolic dimension, based on the condition of stressing the latent aspect of its becoming.

Such skepticism leads us to rethink the figure of the girl in the context of the specific trait that characterizes it: a *uterine infantilization* by which the social body is bound to a potentiality that encodes the circulation of goods. Social groups seem to be fascinated with the idea of an organ whose productive force is latent but promising. This is why they assign the economic function of a normative exchange value to it. This potential demarcates the girl's libidinal geography in a way that will only stop being an exchanged good and become reproductive value when the generated product circulates (by exogamy). The time that elapses between the separation of the girl's body from the mother's and the integration into the body of the women/mothers' collective is a period in which the real value of the body that does not exist becomes speculative.

This is why the girl relates less to the realization of its potentiality of reproduction than to its *non-realization*, because it is only in this state of *latency* that its body acquires a matrix without function, a speculative value, which encodes the libidinal economy of the group. In the parlance of contemporary economic theory, the girl is a *commodity future*, or, to be more precise, it represents future commodification.

The maternal demarcation of the girl's libidinal geography aims to enable the entrance of the girl into the mother's social group. This group is characterized by the actualization of the potentiality of reproduction. This social transfer is achievable only if the girl has been previously *stolen* from and stripped of the mother's body. As a result of this excision, the girl joins a retinue of mothers to make her a woman. A genealogy of girl–mother can be expressed in the following theorem: *the woman* $(0/-)$, the complementary symmetrical stage of the phallus, is the result of the maternalization of the girl. I argue with Freud that the maternal re-instruction of the girl's symbolic body seeks to overcome the castration complex, which takes place when she is being given economic value to a temporary state of being The woman. I argue against Freud, however, that the castration complex begins neither with penis envy nor with the hatred of the mother, but rather in the irreparable symbolic somatic caesura between mother and girl, which determines the anthropogeneric discontinuity between them.

I reframe the archeology of *the woman* in relation to the girl and the mother within the scheme of Freudian psychoanalysis and try to indicate that the action and effect of retaining a matrix in the stage of latency means breaking the laws that mark the anthropogeneric development and evolution. The girl is whimsical under the care of the mother. Once separated from the mother's body in order to follow the evolutionary maxim of becoming *the woman*, she protests against the imperative of transforming her neutral gender from a zero value to the extreme of planning matricide. There is a myth in the history of Western culture that exposes the paradigmatic complexity registered in this uterine affiliation: Electra.

I will develop an archaeology of the feminine through the figure of the girl in relation to the mother. I will show that *the woman* is the result of a language game based on a metaphysical structure that serves the purpose of affirming a single anthropogeneric value: the male. If we refute and reject the logical structures of classical duality, the corollary is that we subsequently do not support the generic status called *the woman*.

a) Sexual maturity of the girl, reproductive capacity and libidinal asymmetry

Both female sexuality and the grammatical neuter have been set up in relation to the male parameters of gender. The incompleteness of female sexuality introduces a third value, but only as a possibility: A girl has the potential to become *the woman* if it enacts an economization of uterine activity. In this sense, the insertion of the girl into the social body of mothers will finally complete the universal value $(1/-)$ by means of isomorphic complementarity.

Thus, there are three processes of determining the femininity of the girl: 1) sexual maturity, 2) reproductive capacity, and 3) libidinal asymmetry. These three factors (re)arrange the libidinal organization, the signifier of the girl's body in order to *speculate* on its potential value and to put it into economic circulation.

Therefore, it is necessary to precisely point out the link between *the woman* and the girl, because, following the Freudian school, being female means putting into circulation an operation of speculative evaluation of uterine potency, the maximum value of which is determined with the completion of the oedipal cycle.

*a.1) When the girl is the absolute difference of the woman,
and the woman is the relative difference of the girl*

In the early stages of the development of the libido, Freud detects a relationship of equality between the boy and the girl.[3] When the phase of sex differentiation begins, at the age of four, the girl begins to differ from the boy, feeling that *something is missing*.[4] It is evident that, according to Freud, the girl's sexual development is completely reduced and subjected to the boy's sexual maturity.

The reciprocal relation says: The girl is clearly distinguished from the boy inasmuch as she lacks that which would realize her libidinal satisfaction. Such theorems subject the girl's impulses and instincts to a dualistic (0/1) and bivalent logic that reduces the proposed mapping of libidinal desire to a passive role[5] and only acquires a generic value

---

3 "Both sexes seem to pass through the early phases of the libidinal development in the same manner. It might have been expected that in girls there were already have been some lack of aggressiveness in the sadistic anal face, but such is not the case. [...] With her entry into the phallic phase the differences between the sexes are completely eclipsed by the agreements. We are now obliged to recognize that little boy is a little man. As we know, this phase is marked by the fact that they have learned how to derive pleasurable sensations from the small penis and connect its excited state with her ideas of sexual intercourse. Little girls to the same thing with their still smaller clitoris. It seems that with them all, according to the mass debate, three acts are carried out on this penile equipment, and that the truly feminine vagina is still undiscovered by both sexes." Sigmund Freud, "Femininity" (1933), *The Standard Edition of the Complete Psychological Works of Sigmund Freud* vol. 22: 1932–1936, trans. and ed. James Strachey (London: Hogarth Press, 1986), p. 3, available at: http://schools.birdvilleschools.net/cms/lib2/TX01000797/Centricity/Domain/1013/AP%20Psychology/Femininity.pdf (accessed: October 31, 2015).
4 "The girl's recognition of the fact of her being without a penis does not by any means imply that she submits to the fact easily. On the contrary, she continues to hold on for a long time to the wish to get something like it herself and she believes in that possibility for an improbably long time; and analysis can show that, at a period when knowledge of reality has long since rejected the fulfilment of the wish as unattainable, it persists in the unconscious and retains a considerable catharsis of energy." Freud, "Femininity," p. 6.
5 "It is not until development has reached its completion at puberty that sexual polarity coincides with male and female. Maleness combines (the factors of) subject, activity and possession of the penis; femaleness takes over (those of) object and passivity. The vagina is now valued as a place of shelter for the penis; it enters into the heritage of the womb". Sigmund Freud, "The Infantile Genital Organization" (1923), *The Standard Edition of the Complete Psychological Works of Sigmund Freud*, vol. 19: 1923–1925, trans. and ed. James Strachey (London: Hogarth Press, 1961), p. 145.

when the girl puts *its* own uterine potentiality into economic circulation.

b) The woman: the maternalization of the girl

We must keep in mind that the semiotization of the feminine is made possible by a social operation, namely that of the insertion of the girl's body into a group of *mothers*. This inclusion determines the temporal economy of latent reproductive power and encodes her libido in the reproductive power and in the economy of care. Only the re-mothering of the girl and the maternal agency of the girl's not-yet-mature organs allow for a grouping within the category of women, which itself symbolizes nothing more than the negative complementary of the male gender (+/1).

As previously demonstrated, the girl–mother relationship does not have to be a pre- or post-oedipal relationship per se. It is important to keep in mind that the mother plays a key role in the oedipal constellation and that, according to the reasoning developed in this chapter, the *woman* is the gendered result of the semiotic re-mothering of the girl's body. The abandonment of the neuter phase and *its* entry into the territory of the feminine is provoked by a re-semiotization of the girl's genital organization and exclusively dependent on the realization of uterine power.

3.
An Irreparable Excision: Mother–Daughter

The girl's genital organization is said to be controlled and dominated by phallic jealousy. *Penis envy* becomes the reason and pretext for humiliating the mother towards the limits of a dispute against her, which aims at a coupling with the father. Thus, the girl will realize her female insufficiency (0/–) and become the symmetrical supplement of the male libido (1/–)—so the Freudian credo would have it.

a) The mother as somatic extension of the uterine space: lap of pampering and pleasure

At an early age, the degree of pleasure is greater than that of libidinal sexuality. The mother is the bearer of pleasure, which is measurable in the mother's provision of food, love, and tenderness within an environment.[6] The nourishing source of pleasure becomes, eo ipso, the first object of love.

The girl and her generic meaning must both be put in relation to the mother, not as an oedipal structure but as a regulating principle that gives context, in the sense of environment and ecology, so that the child can *come to the world*. The mother plays the role of the medium and channel through which the girl experiences the world.

The first mother–child relationships are not oedipal but *environmental* relationships, inter*mediary* relationships, *channeled* relationships, *transferred* relationships through which children experience the world.

The mother serves as a vehicle[7] for both boy and girl through which the child is placed in relation to the world. The mother is the doorway to the outside. and the interaction between mother and child opens up the outside world.[8] She is the first relational object the baby takes as a source of care and pleasure, an environment that lays the foundations for subsequent new objects.[9]

If we were to accept the Jungian objections to Freudian libidinal theory, we would put the mother–girl relationship onto the paradigm Jung indicated in which the mother–child relation is an *object relation* that allows for the opening towards an infinitely vast world (the cosmos). The mother–girl relationship takes us into the heart of the dark continent of psychoanalysis, a foray dedicated to female sexuality, as enigmatic as the societies or cultures Freud called pre-oedipal,[10] located in a layer that comes before the Greek polis.

---

6 Compare Carl Gustav Jung, "The Theory of Psychoanalysis. 6. The Oedipus Complex," *Collected Works of C. G. Jung*, vol. 4: 1906–1916 (Princeton: Princeton University Press, 1970), p. 151–156.

7 William R.D. Fairbairn took a turn from instinct theory to the theory of relational objects. He was joined in this quest by Harry Guntrip, John D. Sutherland, and Donald Winnicott. Object relations theory made it abundantly clear that the relationship with the mother is a privileged relationship. It is a relationship of objects, for only through the relationship with the mother is a child given world experience.

8 Sándor Ferenczi, *Thalassa. A Theory of Genitality*, trans. Henry Alden Bunker (London: Karnac Books, 2011).

9 Carl Gustav Jung, "The Oedipus Complex," p. 151–156.

10 "Our insight into this early, pre-Oedipus phase in the little girl's development comes to us as a surprise, comparable in another field with the effect of the discovery of the Minoan-Mycenaean civilization behind that of Greece." Sigmund Freud, "Female Sexuality," *The Standard Edition of the Complete Psychological Works of Sigmund Freud*, vol. 21: 1931, trans. and ed. James Strachey (London: Hogarth Press, 1986), p. 223–243. Online: http://www.aquestionofexistence.com/Aquestionofexistence/Problems_of_Gender/Entries/2011/8/28_Sigmund_Freud_files/Freud%20Female%20Sexuality.pdf (date of access: October 30, 2015)

b) Rituals of puberty: the girl's separation from her pampering environment and entry into a group of mothers

Each entry into the socio-biological group classified by age takes place through a demarcation on the body by a regime of signs. Castrations, amputations, and semantic extensions on the body carry an irreversible mark that circumscribes the corporal extension in a chain of meanings about the rights and duties relative to the value of life.

Puberty rites have the function of revealing the female genital organization.[11] The rites of menstruation,[12] a sign of a girl's development and sexual maturity, are encoded according to its economic function in the service of society: to be able to fertilize and to reproduce life.[13] Female sexuality is the realization of reproductive capacity. The appearance of menstrual blood indicates speculative value that is assigned to the body of the girl.[14]

The rites of initiation and puberty both serve the organization of female sex, as an anthropotechnical way of splitting the girl from the mother's body, the first act of exogamy. Consequently, the first law of prohibition is that against a mother–daughter fusion.

———

11 These rituals are conducted by covert legions of women-mothers, whose task is to reveal the sign of fertility, a periodic, sacred, and magical force.

12 Compare James George Frazer, "Balder the Beautiful," *The Golden Bough: A Study in Magic and Religion*, vol. 10 (London: MacMillian, 1913).

13 David Graeber wrote the following about the debt system in economies before the existence of money but at a time when "bride prices" were already in existence: "Everyone knew that the only thing you can legitimately give in exchange for a woman is another woman. In this case, everyone has to abide by the pretext that a woman will someday be forthcoming. In the meantime, as one ethnographer succinctly puts it, 'the debt can never be fully paid.' [... W]e are speaking of a human life that also has the capacity to generate new lives." David Graeber, *Debt: The First 5,000 Years* (New York, N.Y.: Melville House, 2001), p. 133.

14 "As mother, the woman remains on the side of (re)productive nature and, because of this, man can never fully transcend his relation to the 'natural.' [...] As both natural value and use value, mothers cannot circulate in the form of commodities without threatening the very existence of the social order [...] The virginal woman, on the other hand, is pure exchange value. She is nothing but the possibility, the place, the sign of relations among men. In and of herself, she does not exist: she is a simple envelope veiling what is really at stake in social exchange. In this sense, her natural body disappears into its representative function. Red blood remains on the mother's side, but it has no price, as such, in the social order; the woman, for her part, as medium of exchange, is no longer anything but semblance. The ritualized passage from woman to mother is accomplished by the violation of an envelope: the hymen, which has taken on the value of taboo, the taboo of virginity." Luce Irigaray, *This Sex Which Is Not One*, trans. Catherine Porter (Ithaca, N.Y.: Cornell University Press), p. 185–186.

Then, we might say that the loss of the neutral girl does not come by her reintegration in matrixial instances (mother–earth, mother–clan, mother–animal). The abandonment of the neutral is the topic of one of the few universal stories told in the history of culture: the separation of mother and daughter, or *endomatrixial prohibition*.

b.1) Mother-daughter schizosoma[15]

The rape of the maiden in the dark caves of the Underworld is an Attic mytheme telling the separation of the daughter from her mother. A girl is running to some remote location where she plays and collects flowers with the daughters of the ocean, then she is abducted by the god Hades. Persephone is the maiden, the mystery, the secret, the victim of the ritualization of sex.

In Eleusis, the divine dimension of the mystery ritual was widely known as *two deities*. They are *the Mother and Daughter*[16]: Demeter, goddess of the harvest, and Persephone, goddess of the Underworld, whose name, according to Homer and other poets, is synonymous with the Maiden Core. Demeter is known for her gift of the ear of grain; there is no secret in the gift, nor in her grief and pain resulting from the kidnapping of her daughter, Persephone. The mystery of the cult of Demeter and Persephone, however, is preserved in the kidnapped girl and carried with her to the underworld to become latent. There, she is brought up and becomes the queen of the underworld. The mother

---

15 The term schizo-soma (χίζειν, schizein, split, splitting and σῶμα, Soma "body") refers to a somatic disorder due to the unfolding of the body. For the development of the body-split affection based on an anthropo-totemic theory, which suggests a development of a gender criterion with the aim of contemplating a signifier of the generic status of the Mother, see Elisabeth von Samsonow, *Anti-Elektra: Totemismus und Schizogamie* (Zürich: Diaphanes, 2007).

16 "At Eleusis the Mystery godhead—I select at first this general form of expression, indeterminate in respect to number and gender—was known to the public as 'the two deities' in a dual form which can mean either 'the two gods' or 'the two goddesses.' [...] Everyone knew that the two deities were *goddesses*. The stress, as far as the public was concerned, was more on the dual. As soon as the initiates entered the sphere of the *aporrheta*, they actually encountered even more deities. And it is not theoretically excluded that in the *arrheton* the *Two* became *One*. In Heredotos the Athenian who explained the miracle to the Spartan before the battle of Salamis mentions no names but says 'the Mother and the Daughter' [...]. The tradition has come down to us that it was Homer and allegedly before him Pamphos, the writer of hymns, who first put 'Persephone,' the name of the daughter, into a poem." Karl Kérenyi, *Eleusis: Archetypal Image of Mother and Daughter*, trans. Ralph Manheim (Princeton, N.J.: Princeton University Press, 1991), p. 28.

feels empowered by her anger about the rape of her daughter and finally obtains the right to stay with her daughter for half a year. It is then that they celebrate the feast of the harvest.

According to the hermeneutic interpretation of the historians of religion,[17] the duality in the female line of the Elysian mysteries—that is, the separation of mother-girl, which illustrates the initiation rite of the girl becoming a woman, the theft of Persephone—helps to explain a cyclical economy of agricultural societies. This cyclical economy involves two assumptions. Mother and daughter are split, dissociated from one another by two complementary forms of symbolic economy: the mother, who perpetuates the woman in reproduction, constitutes her nature as *property*. The girl is nevertheless divided twice, split into the value of the mother and *the woman*, she is exchange value.[18] This ritualization of growing up, the transition from girl to mother is a metaphysical rendering, symbolizing the economy of male desire in which the girl becomes a woman, assigning to (it) her the value of (ex-)change.

4.
Apology for a Crime: Electra (vs. Oedipus)

Electra is a character that, following the reasoning of the article, shows a prolongation of the state of not realizing her uterine potentiality. She dares to rebel against theft and the economy of *uterine agency* by the mother.

Freud frames the narrative of Electra in similar psychological structures as Oedipus, but with one small difference:[19] The reverse

---

17 Compare ibid.

18 Compare Pierre Klossowski, *Living Currency*, ed. Vernon W. Cisney, Nicolae Morar, and Daniel W. Smith (New York, N.Y.: Bloomsbury, 2007).

19 "We have already observed that there is yet another difference between the sexes in their relation to he Oedipus complex. We have the impression that what we have said about that complex applies in all strictness only to male children, and that we are right in rejecting the term 'Electra complex' which seeks to insist that the situation of the two sexes is analogous. [...] Very different is the effect of the castration complex on the girl [...] Only if her development follows the third, very circuitous path does she arrive at the ultimate normal feminine attitude in which she takes her father as love-object, and thus arrives at the Oedipus complex in is feminine form." Freud, "Female Sexuality," p. 223–243. Online: http://www.aquestionofexistence. com/Aquestionofexistence/Problems_of_Gender/Entries/2011/8/28_Sigmund_ Freud_files/Freud%20Female%20Sexuality.pdf, p. 3 (date of access: October 30, 2015).

directionality of the libido, in this case, the hatred of the mother and the love of the father, has to be consumed in *reality*, and only then is the castration complex resolved. The mother is *guilty* of possessing a small and weak, an absent, sex. Only by giving birth, or by taking a husband, may she compensate her deficit.

This leads to a reconsideration of Electra and the artifice of an irreparable distortion of matriarchal societies, transforming them into patriarchal ones. I suppose that the Electra complex does less to show the transformation of matriarchal into patriarchal societies;[20] instead, as Engels says, it shows how matriarchal societies around the world trigger the mother-daughter separation, through which the mother becomes the productive part and the daughter is turned into a commodity of exchange.[21]

Against the thesis that the criminal act of Electra is *a precursor* to phallic envy, I consider it an act not yet contemplated by Freudian psychoanalysis that we will now set up anew as follows: Electra's rage follows from the excision and primary separation of first love. It is directed against *allo-uterine* instances that welcome us once man is expelled from uterine space. The tragedy of the girl must be framed, following Jung, by a fact of rupture within the medial space provided and granted by the matrixial instance, denoting the uterine extension as the *world*.[22]

Clytemnestra's wrath and Electra's exile form a scenario of the *schizosomic* matrixial body; their bodies are separated and semiotized; their uterine power is bi-valued. The mother is productive; she initiates the rites of mourning for her abducted daughter.[23] The girl will be the coin of exchange. In this scenario, might not the act of symbolic hate for the mother mean more than a gesture of *evolutionary disobedience*? Electra does not want to suffer her mother's fate, breaking the chains

---

20 Friedrich Engels refers to this myth in his discussion of the origin of the family, the property, and the State. He states that this myth preserved a transition from a matriarchal to a patriarchal society. See Friedrich Engels, *The Origin of the Family, Private Property, and the State: in the Light of the Research of Lewis H. Morgan* (Chicago: Charles H. Kerr & Co, 1909).

21 See Graeber, *Debt*, p. 137–144.

22 Paraphrasing Jung, the Oedipus complex presents a childhood conflict experienced in adulthood. The affections of children are the results of pleasurable feelings. The *libido sexualis* is articulated only in maturity and according to the social contexts in which the boy or the girl is integrated. The social rules codify the principles of pleasure and sexuality. Compare Carl Gustav Jung, "The Oedipus Complex," pp. 151–156.

23 See Nicole Loraux, *Mothers in Mourning*, trans. Corinne Pache (Ithaca, N.Y.: Cornell University Press, 1990).

that keep her from repeating a future that would forever continue to produce stolen female bodies. We can ask ourselves whether Electra's act may be considered as a suitable gesture of rebellion.

Boyan Manchev

Pandora's Toys, or *zoon technicon* and the Technical Ghosts of the Future

Was Pandora, the motherless first woman, created directly as woman? And what if her immediate creation by the divine blacksmith Hephaestus and the motherless goddess-virgin, the head-born warrior Athena, made her—the future mediator between gods and humans—the paradigmatic figure of immediacy, in other words, of the child?

Pandora, sent to the humans, to the newly-established world of finitude, and therefore of labor, economy and order, had to transgress taboos in order to fulfill her immediate desires. She needed her toys, which the jealous husband-father had locked in the jar. The all-gifted ones always need more gifts. Pandora insists on having her toys.

Let me open this discussion by shortly outlining the critical context at stake. In *The History of Sexuality* Foucault, parallel to Simondon, performs the radical operation of the final denaturalization of the human. Unlike Simondon, Foucault attacks the understanding of sexuality as a new and perhaps last transformation of the eighteenth century's idea of human nature. Foucault recognizes in the Freudian idea of libido the last stronghold of nature understood as profound substratum, which the supernature of the Superego must subdue, purify and master in a Hegelian way. Thus Foucault "liberates" sexuality by historicizing it, by finally submitting it to the subject of history, i.e. revealing it as a historical, cultural and political construct. But Foucault's intention is far from that of Wilhelm Reich, and he deliberately mocks Reich in *The Will to Knowledge*. What is at stake with the attack on the Freudian Trojan horse of nature, the idea of sexuality as nature, is nature itself. As he states in his famous 1971 debate with Chomsky on human nature, in which he attacks the heritage of the eighteenth century through his opponent, justifiably or not, *there is no human nature*.

But even this conclusive attack, this *coup de grâce* on nature, performed by Foucault, which also propelled the upsurge of queer studies, could not cope with the eternal return of nature through the figure of procreation, of biological reproduction. On the contrary, in subsequent seminars, introducing the critical concept of biopolitics, Foucault will still see the ownership of reproduction and reproductive forces as *plastic* substance of power, understood precisely as biopower. The critical analysis of modern biopolitics thus systematically reveals the agencies of *colonization* of the biological, reduced to productive and reproductive potency in the lineage of Marx, systematically put in parentheses in Foucault.[1] Thus, after Foucault—trying to eclipse the problem faced by Foucault, but again according to the logic and the conceptual and ideological dimensions of the horizon established by Foucault—radical feminism and queer studies face the paradox of reproduction: the last and unconquerable stronghold of nature. In this chapter I will attempt to continue with this radical critique along the same lines, without concessions to any late naturalist sentimentalism.

Pandora's Myth

Although philosophers would oppose *logos* to *muthos*, the myth has its own logic. The mythical logic is a complex logic. Its understanding, or at least its conceptual mobilization in the direction of semantically transparent and narratively coherent and articulated meaning, is the object of our own conceptual and interpretative decisions. And yet the mythical logic has powerful symptomatic and heuristic potential. This is why, if the value of this reading method is to radicalize the perspective of historical anthropology in the direction of a figurologi-cal hermeneutics or, more generally, of *fantastic philosophy*, then its *surplus* value would be shining a light on the *unconscious*, dark side of cultural dependencies and structures, persisting to modern times.[2] However, this enlightening operates not mainly through the power of a radiant mythical logos, but through a re-composing of the visible field, laid by the radiance of the unsuspected mythical celestial bodies and fantastic cartography.

Let me generalize a few structural features of the Pandora figure, which could be used for our study of the fundamental perspective, at least in my research, dealing with the relation of technology and the creation of a new body. Pandora is the first known artificial creature: she is an inanimate doll, a statue that becomes alive. However, she is not one of a kind, as Hephaestus produces other *robots*, the *automata* described in the *Iliad*. Pandora, though, is the first artificial creature

---

1 See Michel Foucault, *Naissance de la biopolitique, Cours au collège de France 1978–1979* (Paris, Hautes études, Gallimard-Seuil: 2004); Michel Foucault, *Security, Territory, Population: Lectures at the Collège de France, 1977–1978*, trans. Graham Burchell, (New York, N.Y.: St. Martin's Press: 2007).

2 Among the programmatic texts of historical anthropology see: Jean-Pierre Ver-nant and Pierre Vidal-Naquet, *La Grèce ancienne*. Vol. 1: *Du mythe à la raison* (Paris, Editions du Seuil: 1990); Jean-Pierre Vernant, *The Origins of Greek Thought*, trans. Jean-Pierre Vernant, (Ithaca, N.Y.: Cornell University Press: 1982).

in which the gender difference functions as a distinctive characteristic (thus also the first creature that reveals gender as *artifact*). Pandora is neither divine creature, nor human being, because she is *in between* gods and people. She is *between*, because she is artificial: on the one hand, she is the product of divine technology, but simultaneously she is pro-jected by the gods. She is *projected*—thrown away, *excreted*, like Arachne's thread, thus becoming *automaton*, an autonomous entity. In this sense the figure of Pandora would be the matrix of the anthro-potechnical hypothesis, according to which the human appears from the interstice between the human and its artificial counterpart.[3] But if we read the mythical logic closely, it will turn out that this artificial counterpart is in fact the model of what humanity will subsequently recognize as *human*. That is why the age of humanism and a number of classical authors would consider Pandora positively as the allegory for the *all-giving*, the retro-utopian origin of the human being.[4]

The Autonomized Automata

The idea of *autonomous automata*, technical beings who do not replace slaves but make them obsolete, is not unfamiliar to mythical thought. It logically relates those purely technical beings with the Golden Age, which we conventionally describe through the prism of the humanist and Enlightenment myths as a return to mother nature, in so far as the Golden Age is in fact the time of the direct satisfaction of desires without the mediation of labor, of *work*. (From this perspective it is worth remembering the etymology of the name—*robot*—of the beings invented by Karel Capek in 1920 in his play *R.U.R.* from the word for *work* in Czech *robota*—*labor*.) Such creatures appear both in Ancient Greek comedy, where everyday objects and tools become self-propelled

---

3 We could refer here to the thesis of the Bulgarian theorist and literary historian Miglena Nikolchina: "Thus, the human emerges not through the painful separation of man from animal but through the *entre-deux*, the in-between of man and his own artificial semblance." Miglena Nikolchina, *Lost Unicorns of the Velvet Revolutions* (Fordham University Press: 2012), p. 107. Part of the material of this text is developed in the essay "The New Pandora: Miglena Nikolchina and the Transformation of the Human," published in an anthology dedicated to Nikolchina's 60th anniversary. See *The Parahuman: Grace and Gravitation* [*Парачовешкото: грация и гравитация*] (Sofia: St Kliment Ohridski University Press, 2015).

4 See Dora Panofsky and Erwin Panofsky, *Pandora's Box: The Changing Aspects of a Mythical Symbol* (New York, N.Y.: Pantheon, 1962 [1956]), chap. VI "Pandora, 'Gift of All': Elizabethans and Jacques Callot."

automata,[5] and in Homer's epic in situations that obviously amaze but also have comic potential, as if anticipating Bergson's theses on the comic, inseparable from those by Jentsch and Freud on *The Uncanny*. Hephaestus creates several artificial creatures, from the supporting virgins to the three-legged *robots* (tripods), which travel by themselves to Olympus and back and are tethered to prevent them from escaping.[6] Aristotle also uses the figure of *automata*, which functions as an (in)famous politico-economical allegory. In a famous paragraph of *Politics* he states that even though slavery is not a good praxis, until instruments which propel themselves are invented, slaves will be needed as autopoïetic instruments: "[...] for if every tool could perform its own work when ordered, or by seeing what to do in advance, like the statues of Daedalus in the story, or the tripods of Hephaestus which the poet says 'enter self-moved the company divine,'—if thus shuttles wove and quills played harps of themselves, master-craftsmen would have no need of assistants and masters no need of slaves."[7] Aristotle's reflection, which of course sounds revolting today, is simultaneously extremely modern and mythically archaic, thinking about the necessity for autonomous machines or even autopoïetic machines, as *robots*. The fantastic world of poïetic machines would overcome Pandora's legacy through creating other forms of life, which are self-animating, which are *automata*, just like Dr. Frankenstein's monster is. Here it is, at the end, the creation of Frankenstein itself, the *autonomized automaton*—he too was seduced by the demon of free choice like the robots of Hephaestus.

---

5 In *The Deipnosophists* Athenaeus quotes Crates' *Theria* ("Wild Beasts," 5th century BC): "Each piece of furniture will come when called: 'Come here, table! Set yourself!'" The table will be followed by the knife, the cups, etc. Compare Athenaeus of Naucratis, *The Deipnosophists or Banquet Of The Learned Of Athenæus*, trans. C.D. Yonge (London: Henry G. Bohn, 1854). More on this topic in Alexandre Marcinkowski and Jérôme Wilgaux, "Automates et créatures artificielles d'Héphaïstos: entre science et fiction," *Techniques & Culture* 43–44, *Mythes. L'origine des manières de faire* (2004), ed. Jean-Luc Jamard.
6 "Meanwhile Thetis came to the house of Hephaistos, imperishable [aphthitos], star-bespangled, fairest of the abodes in heaven, a house of bronze wrought by the lame god's own hands. She found him busy with his bellows, sweating and hard at work, for he was making twenty tripods that were to stand by the wall of his house, and he set wheels of gold under them all that they might go of their own selves to the assemblies [agôn] of the gods, and come back again—marvels indeed to see." Homer, *The Iliad of Homer*, trans. Samuel Butler. (Longmans, Green and Co.: 1898), Scroll 18, v. 373–377.
7 Aristotle, *Politics*, 1, 4, 1253b33–1254a. *Aristotle in 23 Volumes*, Vol. 21, trans. H. Rackham (Cambridge, Mass.: Harvard University Press, 1944).

The Anthropotechnical Caesura

Let us return to the (critical) mythical reconstruction of Hesiod.

Hephaestus and Athena's creation is completed under Zeus's guidance, all gods grant tempting gifts, magic crafts and charms to Pandora, *thauma idesthai*, and she is sent to the humans. This moment represents a radical caesura in the history of humanity, which in fact is the beginning of its history *strictu sensu*. Therefore, the divine gift of Pandora to the humans is a *historiogenic* moment. Why? Because, paradoxically, this artificial *creature* is the first mortal woman. Therefore, up to this moment humanity of the Golden Age, consisted solely of men. Being immortal, humanity did not need reproduction. Hence Pandora, the first mortal woman, is not only the first mother, she is also *the mother of reproduction*. She will not only be the mother of the first born and mortal child[8] but something more. She, the artificial creature, comes to introduce and establish what will be perceived as the most *natural* quality of humans as biological creatures, that is to say reproduction. Despite her technical origin, gifted with superhuman powers through the divine technology of the head-*born* goddess-virgin Athena, she, Pandora, is also gifted with this new technology. She is the first (before-/after-) *human* being, who enters into or, more precisely, introduces *the model* of reproduction.

At first glance Pandora, the All-Gifted, does not possess technology, does not have the techno-poïetic mastery and ontological potency of Hephaestus to *produce* things and beings. But we could suppose the following deep structural dependence: Pandora's ability to re-*produce*, to give birth to other mortal beings, is her endowed ability, at one and the same time distancing her but also placing her within structural vicinity, if not in a symmetrical position, to the gods. Because she is an artificial creature, originating from the divine order, she is gifted with this ability, insofar as it is *supernatural*. Pandora is the mother of reproduction as technology.

From this moment, a rupture in the interstice of Pandora is opened up. Between the continent of the gods and the continent of the humans an uncrossable ocean there is. Gods and humans are divided, humans are enslaved by form, colonized by it, while gods keep the potential for a constant transformation of the form to themselves. The result of this

---

8 Symptomatically, the daughter of Pandora is Pyrrha, the only woman who survived the flood, a woman with Titanic genes, of course, who together with her husband Deucalion, son of Prometheus, reproduces again through a magical or quasi-technical operation—through a *miraculous technique*—womankind: throwing rocks behind her shoulders that become women.

technique of reproduction is the repetitive model, which is a reproduction not only of the species but also of the model. This ontotechnical operation *fixates* humankind. Therefore, if we follow the logic of the myth, the first consequence of those structural features of the fable and Pandora's figure will be *reproduction*. At least in this standardized human form it is produced as *technology*.

But if an artificial creature defines the origin of reproduction, we will have to face the consequences of such radical claims. On the one hand, standardized reproduction would appear as a secondary technology compared to the creation of artificial beings through technical mastery. Therefore, reproduction itself would appear as technology; it is a *tekhné*. On the other hand, and this is even more important, in relation to the theses of the entire lineage of political theory, which bases the template of production on the pattern of reproduction, we have to claim that, on the contrary, *reproduction is produced*.

In accepting the phenomenon of production, the archaic insight of Pandora's myth affirms something completely surreal from the modern point of view: production is not based on the model of reproduction, and this could shed a completely different light on anthropotechnics. No matter how paradoxical it sounds, it means nothing less than that reproduction appears in the human world *after* technical creation and, even more surprisingly, after the creation of human beings with the help of technical means. Obviously, according to this archaic logic, which equals highly modern logic, only a technical being can produce this technology, this new form of production, which creates boundaries, therefore finitude, therefore form. And yet, this new technical invention is an anthropogenic caesura. It is the division that enables the gods to remain alone with their eternal potential for changing form. In this sense the invention of the reproductive technique appears as a limit to metamorphosis. Because, let us not forget, there is another production technique that is more archaic than the technique of reproduction, namely the technique of metamorphosis. Before being a process of transformation of form, metamorphosis is the process of the *production* of form, which is the *production* of the body.

From this perspective, it is important to make a clear distinction between the "standardized" form of reproduction established by Pandora and the divine forms of reproduction, which are far from the standard biological matrix. Thus the warrior goddess Athena is *born from the head* of her father Zeus. Dionysus, child of Zeus, is carried to term, partly by Semele and partly by Zeus himself. The archaic logic of the myth suffers neither from phallocracy, nor from *matricocentrism*. The male as well as the female divinities bear and give birth. The divine body does not have a human form; it is a vessel for organs in which holes open and placentas grow in order to give birth to new organs, to new miraculous techniques and new creatures. In this context the myth of Pandora takes a central place. It reveals another form of archaic production, which is neither metamorphosis, nor reproduction, but the production of an artificial body.

Trans before Humanism, or the Plus of the Substance

Long before humanism was born and Erasmus reduced Pandora's *pythos* to a mere *box*, *transhumanism* had already happened. It was a premise and possibility for humanism, insofar as it described the very origin of humankind. Pandora, the technical being establishing the matrix of reproduction, has a technical *matrix*, a womb that, rather than being a jar or box, is, in fact, a vessel, a container—*pan*.

In contrast to the Tertullianian tradition which will be adopted centuries later by humanism, an amateur Hellenistic scholar interprets Pandora as a figure of bitterness, due to symptomatic error. This leads to changing Pandora's gender to "Pandorus." Instead of *omnium munus, the gift of everyone*, the name Pandora/us will be based on "*pan*, quod est totum, et *doris*, quod est amaritudo" ("*pan*, meaning *all*, and *doris*, meaning *bitterness*"). Furthermore, this strange etymology is accompanied by a symptomatic error, revealing the unconscious of the unsuccessful hermeneutic operation: *omnium munus* appears as *omnium minus*, *deprived* of everything.[9] The amateur Hellenistic irritant-of-the-symptom in question is none other than Giovanni Boccaccio with his text *Genealogia deorum gentilium* (On the Genealogy of Gods).

Apart from this symptomatic reading, announcing a technophobia at the dawn of Modernity, my proposed reading is as follows: Pandora, who combines in her body the plastic element of earth, clay, and the dynamic element of fire as well as the *technological* gifts of the gods—all of which lead to the transformative dynamics of the body's origin—will acquire not only the potential of the *automaton* but also the dynamic potentiality for change, for transformation. This will be achieved, on the one hand, through the invention of new technology and, on the other, through the poïetic potential of labor. Labor, incarnated in her by Hephaestus' genes not only as *work* enslaving slaves and robots but also as the poïetic potentiality of exceeding oneself. The human *poïesis*, begun from the compulsion of deprivation, from *penia*

---

9 See Panofsky and Panofsky, *Pandora's Box*, p. 14–15.

and *ponos* inflicted by enduring labor, in order to achieve the technocracy of the *daughter* figures of Hephaestus, from Pandora to Arachne and the statue Pygmalion holds dear.

Pandora, the creature all-endowed by the gods, is not a figure of the *minus*, of the absence (the absence of substance, of spirit, of phallos, of nature, of culture: the Lacanian-Freudian ontologization of absence, predicted by Boccaccio's symptomatic error), but of the *more-than-substance*: the excess of nature, excess of origin, or excess as sole origin—in other words, *technology* or *des-organization*.

By means of the figurological hermeneutics of Pandora's figure, we achieve the possibility of approaching the phenomenon of procreation. This allows us to shed new critical light on attempts to radically reevaluate modern assumptions about *human nature*.

The All-Giving

We should still be attentive to the meaning of the name *Pandora*, the *all-gifted* (Πανδώρα, from πᾶν, pān—i.e. *all*—and δῶρον, *dōron*—i.e. *gift*—therefore the *all-gifted* or the *all-endowed*), which first appeared in Hesiod's *Works and Days*. However, there has been a long-standing tendency in classical philology of reading the meaning of her name in the opposite sense, that is to say as the *all-giving*. This epithet is connected to the archaic provenance of Pandora's figure, structurally close to Gaea and Demeter, the all-giving goddesses of the Earth; a reading serving anthropological and even early feminist ideas, accounting for the possible anthropological dynamics that affect the figure of Pandora and, more particularly, its radical counter-interpretation by Hesiod himself.

I propose instead a complex understanding of the name: a bidirectional possibility of reading of the syntagm Pan-Dora (*all-gifts*): Hesiod's Pandora, Pandora the all-gifted, is nonetheless all-giving, the one giving gifts to everybody (all humans? Or maybe even all gods?). But the gifts she gives to both humans and gods are far from the archaic gifts of Gaea. To the humans Pandora gives form through the possibility of repetition and the production of goods, of autonomous products not given by the gods. Her gift opens the possibility to exceed the archaic economy of a gift. At the same time, she gives their technical gift back to the gods in the form of nature. She gives back the technology of reproduction—a technology that only a technical creature could produce; this new form of production that produces boundaries, therefore finitude, therefore form. If gods produced the agency of finitude, the motherless mother of reproduction, Pandora, produces technology, which makes gods irreversibly immortal, since she opens the time of finitude and thus forces gods to return to their eternal and infinite interchangeability of pleasure and truth. Thus, by growing the technique of procreational reproduction, Pandora, in a way, also gives birth to the gods themselves.

Pandora's Toys

Why, then, does the poet to whom we owe the possibility of this analysis describe this onto-technical agent, this technopoïetic producer—the *producer of reproduction*—as a *bitch* (according to Hesiod, the first woman, the plague for men, had "the mind of a bitch and a thievish nature"[10])?

Of course we could and should be outraged by the fact that this pejorative metaphor is as ancient as the description of the first woman. But it is not an accident in Hesiod's discourse. It would be somehow inadequate to blame Hesiod for being misogynous, taking into account his cultural logic that is completely different to and therefore essentially incompatible with ours. What Hesiod meant by this offense was not the traditional connotation, "a woman with promiscuous behavior," but the fact that Pandora was inactive; she was non-functioning, *désoeuvrée*. She was lazy, inactive; she only wanted to satisfy her own desires, and immediately so, without wanting to work for them. Before describing Hesiod as the father of misogyny or the tribune of patriarchal ideologies, we should take a step back and recognize that, paradoxically, it is precisely the *bitchy* character of Pandora that is significant for her divine substance. She has her insatiable, immediately expressed desire in common with the gods. Therefore, her voracious and insatiable appetite, her anthropogenic substrate, so unflatteringly described by Hesiod, comes from the gods. Being unable to become a metamorphic being herself, lacking access to the *first* technology, which guarantees the immediate satisfaction of the desire, or the overcoming of finitude, she has to cope with the ontological interval yielded by finitude. By other means, she *invents* the technique of pro-*creation* as its substitute. However, she could acquire this technopoïetic capacity only through contact with the first technique. Thus, the first mother was not only a *bitch*. Or, if she had been a bitch, it is because she seemed to be in an infantile state of unproductivity and necessity to

---

10 Hesiod, *Works and Days*, trans. Apostolos A. Athanassakis (2nd ed. Baltimore, Md.: The Johns Hopkins University Press, 2004), line 69, p. 66.

satisfy her immediate desires. But she was like this because she was made by divine hands, and therefore close to the gods, and she was everybody's child, and therefore the *total child*, the *pan-paidos*; precisely for that reason she was the perfect mother as well.

Following his teacher Imre Hermann, Nicolas Abraham claims in *The Shell and the Kernel*, that the mother is creation of the child and therefore the child is the mother of all mothers.[11] The infantile is the meeting point of Hesiod and Hermann and Abraham. In Hesiod the idea is conceived as the infantile state of unproductivity and the immediacy of the motherless creature's desire, the total child Pandora, whereas in Hermann and Abraham it is the reabsorption of the potential of the big *natural* figure of the origin, the Mother.[12] However, following Hesiod's critical version of the myth from Hermann and Abraham's perspective,

---

11 Compare Nicolas Abraham and Mária Török, *L'écorce et le noyau* (Paris: Flammarion, 2009), p. 334.

12 This state of infantile unproductivity, discussed also by Bataille in *Literature and Evil* in relation to Kafka and by Kojève in relation to the end of history, influences, through the mediation of Blanchot's and Nancy's concept of *désœuvrement*, Giorgio Agamben's crypto-substantialist use of the notion as the original state of humankind, on the one hand, and as the messianic state, mirroring the origin, on the other (where, according to Agamben, children will play with the law as with toys). "One day humanity will play with law just as children play with disused objects, not in order to restore them to their canonical use but to free them from it for good. What is found after the law is not a more proper and original use value that precedes the law, but a new use that is born after it." Giorgio Agamben, *State of Exception*, trans. Kevin Attell (Chicago, Ill.: University of Chicago Press, 2005), p. 64. However, Agamben insists that what is at issue is not "a more proper and original use value" (or "a lost original state," as Agamben puts it more succinctly in the last sentence of his book), the trope of playing children inevitably functions as a retro-utopian figure. A brief paragraph in Agamben's *Means Without End: Notes on Politics*, which in commenting on Aristotle's *Nicomachean Ethics* takes up a thesis already formulated in *Language and Death*, suggests the answer to this question, taking it in an unexpected direction: "Politics is that which corresponds to the essential inoperability [*inoperosità*] of humankind, to the radical being-without-work of human communities. There is politics because human beings are *arg s-beings* that cannot be defined by any proper operation—that is, beings of pure potentiality that no identity or vocation can possibly exhaust." Giorgio Agamben, "In This Exile (Italian Diary, 1992–94)," *Means Without End: Notes on Politics*, trans. Vincenzo Binetti and Cesare Casarino. (Minneapolis, Minn.: University of Minnesota Press), p. 140. It turns out that the post-juridico-political or strictly-political state described in *State of Exception* is ultimately conceivable as a restoration of the (lost) essence, of the idea of an anthropological substratum, which is to say, of a figure of human nature (even though it is inverted in a paradoxical way as "inoperative humankind"). For more details on this critical controversy, see Boyan Manchev, *Logic of the Political* (Sofia: Iztok-Zapad, 2012).

we have to realize that the child is the perfect mother not because of its proximity to the natural figure of the origin. It is not the perfect mother as a paradigmatic figure of the natural state of *inoperosità* but as the Master of counter-productive technology (coming from the future).

The child is not the paradigmatic figure of nature. *It* is a technical creature as well. The child is a monster. Therefore, if Pandora is the perfect mother, it is because she is the perfect child.

Queer Temporality. An Epilog to the Future

In order to return at the end to our opening problem, the reproduction of the figure of nature and therefore of reproduction as the natural template of the human, I will tackle Lee Edelman's recent provocative and much-debated thesis, which was one of the last attacks on repro-duction and nature in an almost anti-natalist stance. Outlined in a clear and programmatic way in the article "The Future Is Kid Stuff: Queer Theory, Disidentification, and the Death Drive" (1998) and elaborated further in *No Future: Queer Theory and the Death Drive* (2004), Edel-man's thesis opposes the idea of the future as a horizon of the child and therefore of the teleology of reproductive order:

> [O]utside the cycles of reproduction [...] there are no *queers* in that future as there can be no future for queers. The future itself is kid stuff [...]. Instead we choose not to choose the child, as image of the imaginary past or as identificatory link to the symbolic future [...]; thus what is queerest about us, queerest within us, and queerest despite us, is our willingness to insist intransitively: to insist that the future stops here.[13]

If we go further in the critical perspective opened up by Edelman, we should contest precisely the last relics of the idea of human nature, which I outlined in the beginning as the critical target of this chapter. Edelman's statement, although it is historically and critically valid, could expose us to the risk of a negative reaffirmation of the quasi-ontological character of this situation, although it is socially and cul-turally constructed. In a first phase we can reaffirm this statement unconditionally: Yes, if we critically and politically operate according the logic of the teleological axis of biological time, which is socially constructed as normative, there is no future for queers and there could not be. However, on second consideration such a thesis is hard to

---

13 Lee Edelman, "The Future Is Kid Stuff: Queer Theory, Disidentification, and the Death Drive," *Narrative* 6.1 (January 1998), p. 29–30.

accept from an effectively utopian perspective, because by extension it risks reducing the possibility for queering time itself. The claim that there is no future because the future is to kid stuff would also imply the reaffirmation of a teleological axis of time, which is precisely corresponding to, and the result of, the social convention of reproduction and of certain historical dialectics of family organization and society.

Here I could refer to another crucial moment in Hesiod's *Works and Days*: his description of the five ages of humankind. The first among them is the *Golden Age*, celebrated since by poets and humanists, when men were immortal and there was no reproduction. The decline of the last and worst one, the *Iron Age*, to which the poet himself belongs, and because of which he deplores his fate, will begin when children start to be born with gray hair, when the worm of finitude affects even the colors and the taste of the origin, polluting the innocence of the child. I will designate this last phase of the last generation as the *Uncanny* ratio. There the prosthesis of temporality is inverted. If men are born old, one could assume that while *aging*, they progressively become children.[14] This implies that in the fifth generation the patterns of reproduction would be turned upside down as well. Fathers would not resemble their children any longer, the mimetic thread of affiliation would be interrupted, or, to put it differently, the templates would be *out of joint*. Would children mate to give birth to elderly people? In any case, this uncanny confusion reveals the unbelievable, paradoxical truth that there is no natural origin, that even death could be an origin, a technical origin at that. The uncanny reversal of time reveals the inorganic counter-dynamics of the organic itself.

In Nicolas Abraham and Mária Török's *theory of the crypt* phantoms of the past are coming to possess us. We cannot help but to adjust. In fact, the crypt is found in the future. The future is the space of the crypt, but the crypt is not the space of the *revenants* or *living dead*; it is the space of technical phantoms, technical ghosts. That is precisely why the child is not the horizon of the future. *It* is a technical creature as well. The child is a monster; it is an excess; it is pure becoming. This is the only reason why the future, the space of the technical phantoms, belongs to it.

Yes, we are given the possibility of queering time with the very emergence of techniques. Techniques appear first as agencies of reversibility, which are not superimposed on the vector of biological time but

---

14 Herodot, *Works and Days*, lines 175–200.

intervene in its agency, in its articulation, and they can therefore shift and transform from within the deployment of temporality.

Archaic techniques of metamorphosis are techniques of time production, of temporality, or of the production of structures through which the vector, or the arrow of time, is determined. In fact, metamorphosis appears as the paradigmatic example of the technology of time production—a *chronogenic technology*. Thus, the paradoxical and complex, non-teleological and counter-final temporality of metamorphosis offers the dynamic model, or at least a possibility to think this queer temporality, which not only precedes reproduction but reduces it to one of the forms of producing temporality. Therefore, the time of metamorphosis, its technique of producing temporality, could be perceived as proof that queer temporality exists.

Hence, we could formulate a counter-question to Edelman's: What if the future belongs to robots instead of children? And what if children are themselves robots—uncontrollable, inspiring, and potentially devastating counter-technologies? That is why, we reply to Edelman's melancholic reenactment of the punk slogan *No Future*: Yes to the future, because chaos and contingency, as well as the force of techniques—of bodies-subjects exceeding themselves—will never be reduced to an ultimate and all-consuming *telos*, mirroring the fading fiction of the origin.

Peter Sloterdijk

Theory of Evolution[1]

First Gynecology

The participants in the "Schelling Project"[2] set out from the assumption that every culture—in the strictly ethnographical sense of the term—produces a set of assumptions about the "female facts."

Such "knowledge" is only rarely organized in a "scientific" mode, as, for instance, in the still very rudimentary women's medicine of the Hellenistic period or in current occidental gynecology. In Europe, the latter started taking its currently dominant form after 1800. It has the traits of a well-defined, academically clinical discipline inasmuch as it is rooted in the principles of experience, experimentation, and compatibility with related theoretical milieus, particularly biology, chemistry, and physics (compatibility). Such knowledge virtually never takes the shape of a philosophical system. Should this anomalous case occur, one has every reason to study it more closely. More details about this below.

What one commonly knows about women's issues—physiologically, psychologically, ritually, aesthetically, biographically, and so forth— and what one hears in everyday culture, can be categorized as partly

---

1 This text is an excerpt from Peter Sloterdijk's philosophical novel, *Das Schelling-Projekt. Ein Bericht* (Frankfurt am Main: Suhrkamp, 2016).

2 Here and in the following pages, this keyword identifies the research project that explores the biosocial premises of the female sexual experience in the period between the Paleolithic (or the Middle Paleolithic, 200,000–40,000 years) and the present day in light of the hypothesis that the experience of pleasure is progressively subjectivized or personalized. References to the German Late Idealist philosopher Friedrich Wilhelm Joseph Schelling (1775–1854) have a more emblematic than monographic character in this context. They do not intend to make a contribution to Schelling studies, which follow suit to Peter Xavier Xiliette's impulses from the 1980s and 1990s. Rather, we want them to be considered impulses for cultural sciences in general and for the humanities, which have to put up with the allegation of engaging in institutional masturbation and methodical autism, thus having lost their connection to the standards of a global discussion of natural sciences and life sciences decades ago.

An application for the support of this venture was submitted to the German Research Foundation in Bonn under the title, *Between Biology and Human Sciences: The Problem of Developing Heterotic Sexuality on the Way from the Hominid Female to Homo Sapiens Women from an Evolutionary Perspective under Constant Consideration of the Natural Philosophy of German Idealism*.

serious, partly humoristic stereotypes. "Knowledge" of this kind never exceeds the status of episodic observation. Family lore and private mythologies fall into the same category inasmuch as they offer concepts that are fit for everyday use. In this field, one knows as much as one credits oneself with having learned. Usually, there is no reason to be held accountable for individual pieces of information.

Knowledge pertaining to women, therefore, is always dogmatically worded, as long as one understands it as the use of an assertion that does not require explanation. From the perspective of everyday knowledge studies (*connaissance ordinaire*, folk knowledge), each member of a homo sapiens group is equipped with a quantum of "feminological competence." Human existence irrefutably encompasses "knowledge" pertaining to women. (Instead of knowledge one ought to speak of "cognitive particles.") Whether there are innate ideas alias genetically determined "cognitive modules" requires further investigation. Our proposition ought to steer clear of the quicksand of the innate ideas debate as long as possible.

"The woman" belongs to the "objects" or "topics" or "enunciative fields" with regard to which total opinionlessness would be impossible. An infant is already "experienced with women," although it does not show it at first. One cannot know nothing about "the woman," no matter how drenched in clichés the ostensible "knowledge elements" may seem under closer scrutiny. One day, the duke will sing "La donna è mobile," and the couples in the pit will give each other a quick smiling glance.

Observations of this kind generate a definition: The human being—male, female, intersexual—is an animal condemned to know women. Human beings unavoidably know too little about women—but also bewilderingly too much. Consequently, they are generally creatures disappointed by women. As always, disappointment is the just wages of prejudice. One participant remarks that "gynecognosis" has a tendency towards tragedy.

(The term, introduced into the debate by Guido Mösenlechzner, does not meet with the participants' general approval. One does not want to disavow its ingenious tendency, but the word creation might have the disadvantage of grossly overvaluing the subject. Silbe quotes Plessner: Nothing can be expected of overarching constructs, except their collapse.)

At this stage of the discussion, Sloterdijk starts an impromptu speech in which he points out that Lorenzo da Ponte, Mozart's Viennese librettist during the 1780s, had Leporello merely pretend to list his master's lovers in the Catalogue Aria in the first act of the opera *Don Giovanni* (which premiered in Prague in late October 1787).

In truth, Don Giovanni's servant designed a document in which every male person would be able to make a list of his encounters with members of the fair sex, regardless of whether their origin was domestic or foreign. Desire, as we know, is not always patriotic; erections frequently have a treasonous streak. Moreover, the list is not so much about conquests resulting in penetration than about all instances of being touched by the other sex.

"Madamina, il catalogo è questo:" Untouched by the others' skepticism, one panelist claims that there is no man on Earth, irrespective of his vocal range, who is not allowed to use this phrase to begin building his rapport about impressions of the female world. From countertenor to bass, all male voices operate in the sphere of catalogues.

To the panelist, the manner in which Leporello fills out the form for his master only concerns us, who are outside the opera, indirectly. The aria's phrasing delivers nothing more than a local example of a unilaterally erotomaniacal list. Based on its textual direction—that much can be admitted—Leporello's register counterbalances the incidents of the punished brute with a perplexingly large number of female characters of European origin, which, by the way, may give rise to the assumption that Turkish women become European as soon as they come within the reach of Don Juan's energy.

One should read Leporello's form in a much more radical way: It is neither an index of successes nor a chronicle of sins. It is construed in such broad terms that it is capable of documenting all informative cases of male closeness to the female world. It is a breviary of touch.

Il catalogo è questo, indeed. If one were to understand the catalogue in sufficiently general terms, it would inevitably begin at a very intimate place for all concerned. It registers the intrauterine heartbeats of the mother, which result in the rhythmic modes of classical and popular music; it ends with the night nurse's handshake at the hospice, who asks you upon your departure from existence if you have anything to declare.

In short, the problem of cataloguing ranges farther than small-minded Mozart aficionados are willing to grasp. If ardently Catholic Spain is the place where one thousand and three affairs are recorded for the indefatigable hero of penetration, the message behind this number simply cannot be ignored.

What was this fairytale number to prove? Nothing but that this sun-burnt nation's ladies acted much more cliché-driven at the time than other beauties between the Volga and the Atlantic. Already in Don Juan's lifetime, Spanish ladies were on the verge of a nervous breakdown. Their yearning for the moment of subjugation had a religious tint, as was still customary for the time. From a cultural-historical point of view, it remains remarkable how a blossoming female population could be seized by the phantasm of the erect Christ.

The exception also bears mentioning. Nobody has thus far thought about the significance of da Ponte listing the ironically low number of one hundred conquests in France. No less than two hundred and thirty successful amorous skirmishes in Alemagna, although German women—with the exception of the Apple Queens from the North and Rhinelanders—had the reputation of pressing their lips together as soon as masculine eyes glanced upon them. We had better say nothing of Italian women. Leporello reports of no less than six hundred and forty entries in his master's Italian list, which, incidentally, may be proof enough that our Spanish hero engaged in a Mediterranean-influenced predatory preference not far from erotic racism. The ninety-one mountings of female servants of the Ottoman Empire are not enough to relativize the report.

In the panelist's opinion, it is time to interpret the numbers' message correctly! Ninety-one Turkish women *en passant* and merely one hundred in France, the supposed motherland of seduction? Who could ignore this rise of the modern gender war in the statistical mode?

The puzzle's answer is unmistakably incorrect. Already in Mozart's and da Ponte's lifetime, word got around that French women displayed an off-putting jitteriness both in erotic matters and in general. Naturally, the jittery ones claimed to pave the way for women's emancipation. It is certainly true that, at the time, the fair generation in the land of Thérèse the Philosopher already read treatises on machine people, the grain trade, checks and balances, and abortion. They considered the use of the bidet Article One of the *droits de la femme*. Which makes it easy to understand why the Iberian omnivore tended to avoid French women.

He steered clear of these representatives of femininity as much as possible, even though he, by some accounts, would otherwise not even shy away from ugly creatures, as long as they wore a skirt. Leporello had thought of everything: the skinny one (magrotta) in the summer, the fat one (grassotta) in the winter, and the old hags throughout the year, just for the pleasure of having them on the list.

Da Ponte, the panelist concludes, was therefore unmistakably a scumbag. He put the conviction in Leporello's mouth that a woman's true place was in the vicinity of the erect redeemer. In a certain way, Mozart was complicit by providing his heavenly indifference in order to elevate this dubious episode from the eternal drama of the sexes to immortality. Cento in Francia! This insult was to have consequences. The second sex beyond the Rhine waited for the twentieth century to take revenge on Don Juan for his fugacious interests.

Apparently it escaped Sloterdijk's notice that his colleagues let him continue to speak just to be polite. He remained steadfast on the course of his digression.

He continued to argue that Leporello's records were ultimately super-fluous as soon as one put looking and touching so close together as to comply with the phallic psyche. Is not the eye a tactile organ as well? Each visit to a large city may attest to this. Just go to Madrid's Atocha railway station in the morning or to the Puerta del Sol at sunset. In just one hour, you will be passed by so many women in full command of their most stimulating sexual characteristics—in a work-related hurry or promenading in the Madrilene evening—that trying to do justice to each individual appearance would make you dizzy. Each in her own way will represents a negligence. Of course, you would only rarely yell after one who hurries away: "Oh you, who I would have loved; oh you, who knew it!" You would be left alone with your countless silent declarations of love. The number one thousand and three is a symbol of missed opportunities to declare your love.

From his disciplinary perspective, Mösenlechzner adds that Don Juan basically knew very little about women, that he actually did not want to know anything about them except that all of them would imag-ine to be the person for whom he, the eternally restless one, had been unsuccessfully searching. What one calls seduction is always a form of transaction in which two speculations intertwine. The man accepts it when the ladies want to instantly redeem him in order to redeem them in turn, and the women allow the hero to transition to the fugue without a prelude. The seducer and the seduced have nothing of which to accuse each other, provided that they realize that is just as immoral to unfetter a woman as it is to want to redeem a man.

Sloterdijk still, who repeats himself: Leporello's catalogue only appears to be a list of sexual incidents and is rather the sum of events in which awareness of the feminine expands. Awareness and knowledge of this kind are largely independent of physical touch. The physically touched woman is much less different from the physically untouched woman than one might assume. Sloterdijk quotes the cynical young Brecht: The face is different; their knees are all weak.

This might be the place for remembering the otherwise suspect distinction between sex and gender. Generally, looking and listening is sufficient to breathe fresh air into the corpus of the knowledge of women. Paying attention to the noise of published opinions contrib-utes to the animation of the anecdotal pool.

Therefore, gynecology—as the unspecified discourse about "the woman" or "women"—represents a massive layer in the national wealth of prejudices in all cultures. This is no different for men than for women themselves. There is a schoolyard gynecology and a tavern gynecology, a gynecology of the factory halls and a gynecology of the party convention, a gynecology of the swimming pool and a gynecology of summer festivals (both highly cleavage-oriented), a gynecology of the shopping mall and a gynecology of women's magazines. All varieties can be objectified by way of in-depth interviews and media excerpts. Language games pertaining to women refer, in a vaguely encyclopedic fashion, to the combined total of the *fait féminin* as a subset of the *fait social*.

All panelists agree that a high factor of misjudgments resonated in the discursive jostle about all things feminine. It seems as if the subject of the "woman" was an invitation for vainglory, polemics, and delirium. Few other subjects of human discussion impose on opinion holders a tendency for impertinence with such great rigor. The tendency far exceeds that which is commonly understood as bias. The subject unleashes forces that bear witness to an elementary tendency towards distortion. One would almost have to suspect a "passion for missing the point." Mösenlechzner stressed the almost irrefutable persistence of stereotypes pertaining to women. And yet, their validity should not be underestimated. Not infrequently, they possess a momentum of their own for prophecies that make themselves come true. Whatever one babbles on about, sooner or later applies.

With respect to women's issues Sloterdijk makes the point that an intercultural pathos of misjudgment comes into play that may best be interpreted using Nietzsche's theorem of the will to non-knowledge, which manifests itself in the form of a dual flight: from disappointment to the ideal and from the ideal to cynicism.

There is unanimity among the participants with regard to the long-term effects of "gynecologies:" Speeches on women are entropic; sooner or later, they all culminate in banality. Where idealizations disintegrate, many who are disappointed withdraw to the ostensibly hard facts: pure copulation, without the added value of affection and metaphor.

Mrs. Stutensee argues that analogous observations could also be made about the speeches about man and men. Just like there is no agynecological "society," there is also no andrology-free society. A permanent civil war of speeches, counter-speeches and counter-counter-speeches rages on the field of gender difference. Gender and sex share the property of constituting empires of half-truths, entrenched behind almost impossible positions. It is very difficult for more profound knowledge to stem fortifications of this kind.

In contrast to the marketable varieties of speaking about women's issues, there is one single form of discourse about femininity in Western civilization that eludes public knowledge and its pathological and satirical motives from the outset. This discourse constructs female fact out of ontological principles and (where they are objectively unavailable) out of terms from natural history. This observation applies exclusively to the natural philosophy of German Idealism, influenced by Schelling (1775–1854), which is closely connected to the contemporaneous evolutionism.

As is generally known, its origins date back to 1800, when Schelling distanced himself from his mentor Fichte (1762–1814). To us panelists, Schelling's "immortal insight" consisted in prepositioning a material history to the Fichtean exposure of the self-generating ("setting") ego.

Fichte had discovered that the ego behaved like a model: At first it strikes a pose, then it gives its reflection the permission to copy it. The pose must be complete; the images follow. This requires the ego to know itself before it makes something of itself. Its first gesture is not a reflection but a self-confirmation. I am familiar with myself, therefore I make myself; I make myself, therefore I am. Schelling then wanted to take things a step further: He brought into play a natural basis of ego-setting (of posing ability) without which all expressions such as ego, self, subject–object, Be-ing, life, and the like would slip into incomprehensibility. In order for me to execute the pose of being myself, there must already be something about me that can move on its own accord. As a member of nature, I am already there before I am there. I seem to be the eye of a needle through which truth must fit, provided it wants to come to light. Is it any wonder that there are long lines waiting in front of my ego?

Schelling's original insight is essential for our project. It is based on the argument that a non-ego-like thing is a prerequisite for the being-able-to-be-there of an ego—call it an organism, body, sentient frame, existence, nature, inner heat, will, drive towards expansion, or whatever.

A thing of this kind can consist of the functional community of trillions of cells. Incidentally, "cell" is an architectural metaphor that transitioned from the religious sphere into biology. It is something in which a monk dwells, comparable to a separate substance. Countless cells want to form a community, similar to an overcrowded monastery, whose community prays to a life turned ego.

The thing that constitutes the living organism has been feverishly awaiting its awakening in a subjective locale since prehistoric times—whether one calls it consciousness or ego or self is of no consequence at first. In Schelling's philosophy, the dark pre-ego bears the seemingly worn-out but actually splendidly refurbished name, nature. Consequently, nature must be understood as something that since time immemorial has been underway to a coming-to-itself in an ego-like focus.

Such a point can only always light up "in myself." Depending on the context, milieu, epoch, and disposition, one might call this ego-like focus consciousness, soul, Christ, Ātman, psyche, God's spark, microcosm, being-there, or global collection point. That which is called warm-bloodedness in relation to the animal body corresponds to the feeling of being-there in relation to the warmth center of Being. That which senses that it exists, lives as an ontological endotherm, as a he, as a she, or as a median. Over the course of millions of years, evolution heats up the conditions of being inside. The rest of the world reacts by accepting the invitation to introduce itself to the well-tempered, irritable interior.

Pathetic turns cannot be avoided beyond the critical threshold. Nature opens its eyes as unconscious unpassed past within humans, if one takes them philosophically seriously: With these optics it looks within itself and pans the exorbitant whole that it represents for itself and in itself. When it is then perplexed, it finally and really comes closer to itself. Thought finds its cause in the horror, in the dark mode of astonishment. Schelling occasionally speaks of a "nameless terror in nature."

Human beings are the means to nature's autopsy. They are the eyes of Being and, at once, its blindfold. The opened eye must shudder at what it sees, for what it initially sees before it is the boundless desert of the past. Being is the sum of all of freedom's victories and defeats. It could have all gone differently, but now it is the way it is on hand.

In human beings, nature is ashamed of itself. Shame is the book of nature's silent proofreader. How could I have given in to the urge to explain myself based on nature?

Old Being has become eccentric ever since it got involved in becoming-human. It increasingly sets itself next to itself: Should I forever be and remain what I was? Doesn't the disgrace of Being become more unbearable the longer it lasts? Don't Being and being-degenerate ultimately amount to the same thing? Should I ever have had anything to do with Being in the first place?

I, spawn of nature, hereby distance myself from that which I have been to this moment. Let the Being-trolls act out in whatever way they please! In the future, I want to belong to the other side; I defect to the camp of free tasks. I don't want to lie there like a garbage bag on the landfill of Being. I want to be different from Being.

Translated by Georg Bauer

KARIN FERRARI *weird wired viral*

```
dot gain photoshop                    →
```

LEO.org - Ihr Spra...   Fantasia Monarch ...   Decoding Azealia ...   23 Tips From Com...

Upload

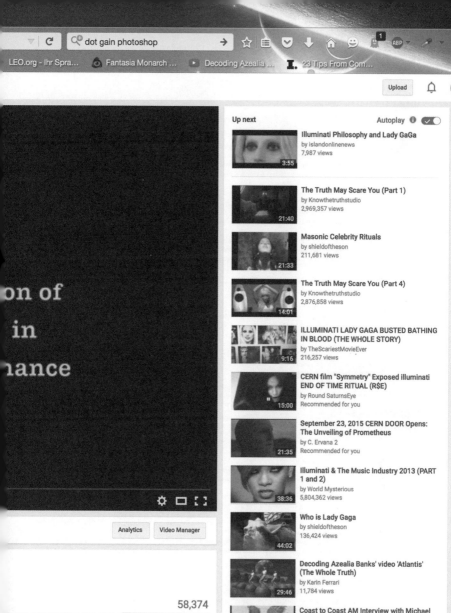

Up next   Autoplay

Illuminati Philosophy and Lady GaGa
by islandonlinenews
7,987 views
3:55

The Truth May Scare You (Part 1)
by Knowthetruthstudio
2,969,357 views
21:40

Masonic Celebrity Rituals
by shieldoftheson
211,681 views
21:33

The Truth May Scare You (Part 4)
by Knowthetruthstudio
2,876,858 views
14:01

ILLUMINATI LADY GAGA BUSTED BATHING IN BLOOD (THE WHOLE STORY)
by TheScariestMovieEver
216,257 views
9:16

CERN film "Symmetry" Exposed illuminati END OF TIME RITUAL (R$E)
by Round SaturnsEye
Recommended for you
15:00

September 23, 2015 CERN DOOR Opens: The Unveiling of Prometheus
by C. Ervana 2
Recommended for you
21:35

Illuminati & The Music Industry 2013 (PART 1 and 2)
by World Mysterious
5,804,362 views
38:36

Who is Lady Gaga
by shieldoftheson
136,424 views
44:02

Decoding Azealia Banks' video 'Atlantis' (The Whole Truth)
by Karin Ferrari
11,784 views
29:46

Coast to Coast AM Interview with Michael Salla and Corey Goode (9-14-15)..
by loowingbwoa
Recommended for you
1:15:51

LADY GAGA SHOCKING ILLUMINATI CONFESSION
by axis4peace4
355,522 views
4:17

BEYONCE QUEEN OF ILLUMINATI
by IlluminatiREVO
1,012,405 views
2:57

Lady Gaga : clip satanique Illuminati subliminal expliqué (2/2) "Bad
by GHETTO LIBRE
107,515 views
10:20

on of

in

nance

Analytics   Video Manager

58,374

👍 177 👎 46

omance by Lady Gaga shows her initiation that consits of her
ne sun, which, as an astronomical body, is actually a star. The

Top-Kommentare ▼

BaptizedN Blood vor 1 Monat
Nice analysis!
Antworten · 1 👍 👎

Kristen Francis vor 2 Wochen
So bizarre.
Antworten · 1 👍 👎

Natalie Spa vor 6 Monaten (bearbeitet)
I don't agree with all the interpretations but interesting none the less. They failed to mention the bald cat is a mutant called a Sphynx, plus the diamond scene is a reference to 'time travel' in a sense or at least the freezing of time & suspended animation which would have occurred as a result of her programming and/or mutation. The animal heads on the wall of the bedroom are both male by the way. Suspended animation is a very real phenomenon.
Antworten · 1 👍 👎

Joker Amatullah vor 7 Monaten (bearbeitet)
After i've researched illuminati through some years, i always realize that, the songs has never to do anything with the music video at all....
The same with Katy Perry with Dark horse. A black magic, witch song, with ancient egypt music video. The only thing they have in common, is, that in ancient egypt, in Moses' time (peace be upon him), they practiced alot of magic.
But else, two different things. And the funny is, Katy Perry performed exactly, the way it should be, that matches her song, WHICH a satanic ritual....
Antworten · 👍 👎

Brigid Imbolc vor 6 Monaten
I think it is a very good analysis! But of course there are a lot of great artists behind this video, expert in symbolism, story etc...
Lady gaga does what she is asked to do.
Antworten · 👍 👎

KiLLuMiNaTi 93 vor 10 Monaten
She just depicts that she sold her soul ..
Antworten · 👍 👎

Carter palmer vor 1 Jahr
LEAVE MOTHER MONSTER ALONE
1 👍 👎

Chawchi Machado 1 year ago
So much BS in one video. I couldn't help but laugh, there are a dozen of other videos all claiming to breakdown the symbolism behind Gaga's videos, and I think this is better than stand up comedy, i laugh so muh. Hahahahaha
Reply · 3 👍 👎

Hide replies ∧

Courtney Couture 1 year ago
Maybe you should pay more attention to the shit around you. It's no coincidence these symbols are plastered all over oth music videos, movies and tv shos. As the old saying goes, you see only with your eyes, so you are easy to fool.
Reply · 2 👍 👎

Chawchi Machado 1 year ago
I have payed attention to all of them, and apparently you did not understand that this is what I was talking about, there are many symbols and so many different ways of interpreting these symbols and even more people that claim what they are saying that all of this becomes a bunch of bogus rethoric. It is impossible that all of them are right, and it is extremely fu to see how they go at each other's throat
Reply · 1 👍 👎

mark mill 1 year ago
lady gaga doing these things on purpose? lol. she could be programed to sit in symbolic positions like that tho.
Reply · 👍 👎

TheReporter5000 10 months ago
You watched **evidence** and all you can do is make fun of it... I feel sorry for you, you are lying to yourself because you do want to believe the truth and you want to stay comfortable.
Reply · 👍 👎

reknaren03 11 months ago
Where did you get all dis info? I'm amazed!
Reply · 👍 👎

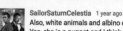

SailorSaturnCelestia 1 year ago
Also, white animals and albino ones in particular, are considered sacred to God Yahweh and so Satanists kill them as a sacrifice!
Yes, she is a puppet and I think she's meant to die early like Amy Whitehouse because all the things she has always said indicate
it! Love to you, Stephanie, I pray lots for you!
Reply · 👍 👎

Lolafabiola85 1 year ago
If you're a grown adult calling yourself a "little monster", seek therapy.
Reply · 4 👍 👎

R. Fiv. 1 year ago (edited)
this sharp analysis of the video can be part of a 'therapy' not to be alienated but to gain distance.
Reply · 2 👍 👎

salford Pirro 1 year ago
the bitch will pay for her sins
Reply · 2 👍 👎

angelsarereal777 1 year ago
Good job you took your time and tried to break everthing down.
Reply · 👍 👎

Kelvin Bong 1 year ago
Now I understand what the music video was showing us thanks! I only liked the instrumental version anyway
Reply · 👍 👎

Kevin Rushton 1 year ago
There sure is a lot of cleverly crafted crap like this you have to sort through while looking for good music to listen to....
Reply · 👍 👎

TheTricye1 1 year ago
You know Lady Gaga came from an ancient deity Lady Nada
Reply · 👍 👎

a./ 1 year ago
"666" is clearly explained in scripture: it is the number of the name of the BEAST.
1 👍 👎

shewa gacy 1 year ago
they try to educate us in their initiation ...cool but any way i love lady gaga much much
Reply · 👍 👎

Kayla Q 1 year ago
Lol! I love it how people get offended so easily! XD But seriously, Gaga is a disgusting W and apart of the Illuminati. I really don't
care if this comment has offended anyone. :)
👍 👎

MrOpportunityknockin 1 year ago
I couldn't said that any better. Thank u
1 👍 👎

Pokemonkid432 1 year ago
Its not her fault. She is nothing but a brainwashed slave
2 👍 👎

Kristel Knight 1 year ago
U know alot.. o.o
Reply · 4 👍 👎

Penelo555 2 years ago
someone had time to spend...

electron maker 2 years ago
Oh God:(

YorktownUSA 3 years ago in reply to GADY LAGA
why?

Daniel Spencer 2 years ago
They arent saying g Lady Gaga is evil, or satanic, they showing tonnes of highly likely hidden messages etc, calm your tits monsters. This is REALLY interesting.

Brandon Young 3 years ago in reply to LunaSeaSane
Or.... crazy thought, 119 bpm is very common for pop music/disco music which is a style of music Lady Gaga uses a lot. Plus Pokerface and Just Dance are around the same tempo as well.

Hailey Babi 3 years ago
Very thorough.

anonymouseketeamster 3 years ago
Excellent analysis. Well done. :)

GADY LAGA 3 years ago
I STILL LOVE HER

Rafa Peña 2 years ago
Vaya paja mental

william randolph 2 years ago in reply to Moattez Ykhelfoune
you are a puppet, child

jaocb hughes 2 years ago
She sacrificed herself for the fame, the power to rule the world.

Rogan Tydd-Whiting 2 years ago
the dog isnt a symbol of egyptian gods thats Lady gaga's dog, she used to have two they were in lots of videos pre born this way the vodka is in the video cause its in a russian bath house and the sun passing through it looks cool. i cant even watch this entir video... someone spent way too much time grasping at thread on this one

LunaSeaSane 3 years ago in reply to Brandon Young
Defend her all you like. In all likelyhood, she's getting all those ideas from Stanley Kubrick who used numerology basedl time co in his films.

sarah habbo 2 years ago
LIVE MY MOTHER MONSTER ALONE >x(!! Little monster for ever !! >:)

B Mob 2 years ago
Well done! Its making so much more sense to me now, all puppets have an "initiation" just got to look for it, and this is Gaga's I would say.. Officially controlled...

luisgdjr 3 years ago in reply to hkq999
@hkq999 Lord willing, the Holy Spirit has more time to lead unbelievers to Christ to avoid the 'strong delusion' to come. i really think we are nearer than most think. i suppose so much time has lapsed that most think it is all a myth. chooose Jesus Christ!

Madolia Steel 2 years ago
Oh well....we believe that the these white coffins in the begining are for 'the Children of the Night' cause GaGa is using quite so creepy and vamp things...

Kahlia Gadsden 2 years ago
Yo Lady GaGa is a scary A Bitch.

Zack Royster 2 years ago
Thumbs up to The person who made this video.

theN4ever 2 years ago in reply to dvdert6
Are we just ignoring the occult symbolism now? they are making her the talk of the town because they have an agenda. Weird weird. If they just wanted her to be famous by being weird there would be no need to load avdeo with disturbing elements. She glorifying evil and bad things and that is that is the art of deception my friend. Open your eyes. You are justifying this because don't want to see the truth. I used to be a fan but I woke up. I gave up this music to save my soul

Makayla Feldman 2 years ago
Lady gaga is shady as crap. Very sketchy video.

Chan Baller 3 years ago
14:52 reverse 6's on computers and head phones

luisgdjr 3 years ago

i'm done listening to this song because of the spiritual root (aka ear worm) effect it has, but another thing that i noticed about it: if you are sucked into the chorus and it takes root... it doesn't take too many runs before the words start sounding a lot like "i don't want Your love, i want Your revenge, you and me, god's a baphomet." Jesus Christ help us... save us, in Your divine grace!

Neal Adam 2 years ago

These videos are interesting.
Both lady GaGa's and this interpretation!
Have fun lady gaga, if you read this.

thepatient08 3 years ago

People who call this stuff nonsense are truly blind. Something so well orchestrated and carefully planned is stuffed to the risers with weirdness and symbolism, yet they ignore it.

luisgdjr 3 years ago

thank you for sharing... i don't know who you are and if this is your original video, but this along with her involvement of ringing in new year's in time square has me so convinced of how near we are. i want to hear from Jesus regarding this and what needs to be done between now and His coming. for now, i suppose the obvious... warn everyone and plead with the unsaved.

haisooni 2 years ago

it is an amazing and deepest interruption for the "bad romance" video clip. Thank you so much.

ccassandra9 2 years ago

You know you can't come on youtube without this illuminati crap it's getting old and quite frankly it's silly. You are trying to tell me there is a worldwide secret society controlling everything when we know your left hand couldn't keep a secret from your right hand and btw you people posting this stuff makes more people watch it and they have figured out this sells so blame yourselves. All this deep interpretation is bullshit i don't think these people are that smart.

Standard 33 2 years ago

666 is the mark of the beast not somekind of sun number open your eyes

gelbabigel 2 years ago

It still feels reductive

Kyng Mania 3 years ago

Actually the origin of that symbol means love in intelligence in sign language ;]

C0rr0d3r 3 years ago

great work!

Kyng Mania 3 years ago

Also the balphomeat!!!!! IN REAL LEGEND is a neutral creature who HATES the devil, but hates god.

Kyng Mania 3 years ago

The -P- means political preference of auctioning you dumb shit.

spidermarcus 3 years ago

Pray to the Fischgod!!!

supercakes09 3 years ago

la loi, c'est moi means in french "the law, it is me."

InfamousValdon 2 years ago   in reply to Cesar Alvarez

Your out of your fucking mind. Leave "Mother monster alone" ?What? What the fuck is a "Mother monster" This bitch is off her rocker. She should be called "Satanic Weirdo" I had no idea stating an opinion was bullying. Grow up and get off the bathsalts. She's obviously heavily into drug, alcohol, gay sex and straight up weird shit. If you wanna idolize this freak, be my guest. This bitch is a skid mark on the underpants of humanity, just like her followers. And. Go fuck yourself.

spidermarcus 2 years ago

Go Postal!

Estefisosa84 3 years ago

Bad Romance????? hmmmm it sounds like.... Baphomet.....

Hathor Bast 2 years ago   in reply to R.i.C

Two words: SHUT UP.

Zack Royster 2 years ago

I'm just now realizing to

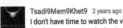

Tsadi9Mem9Khet9 2 years ago
I don't have time to watch the video, nor to read the comments, so excuse me if this has been mentioned, but here's a translation of the Gaga-ese part at the beginning and throughout the song: "Ra Ra Ah-Ah-Ah" translation: "I am not a Ra worshipper" "Roma Roma-ma" translation: "I am a Roman Catholic."

gina2190 3 years ago
EXCELLENT MORE TO THIS THAN FIRST HITS THE EYES

theN4ever 2 years ago in reply to Standard 33
The mark of the beast has an origin that is not specified in the Bible. 666 has other meanings and people use those to subliminal embed it. They hope we'll be accustomed to seeing son that when the big reveal comes people will willing accept there plans. A sense of familiarity and ,as we all know, people are more accepting of things they're familiar with.

Sultana S. 3 years ago
good work, please check my version of the Gaga Doll

hiscash 3 years ago
Man... Deep.

LunaSeaSane 3 years ago in reply to LunaSeaSane
AND:
11:05 Watch her lips, slightly off sync; good chance she's not saying
"bad romance"... but "baphomet".

Kyng Mania 3 years ago
Paganism isn't related to satanism...

Firstname Lastname 2 years ago
She's not all that bright just greedy, so who taught her all this? Who's behind it?

Gerard McCurley 2 years ago
Boring video

GADY LAGA 3 years ago
THAT IS WHY ILLUMINATI GAVE HER 400 MILLION VIEWS BECAUSE SHE IS AN EVIL GENIUS

Dominique Mayfield 2 years ago
I dont believe any of this but it is very interesting. Im sure Lady Gaga would be proud to the attention to detail and your interpretation of her art.

OscarBravo 2 years ago
Gaga for the win.

Moattez Ykhelfoune 2 years ago
Bitch please, been a fan doesn't mean i'm an illuminati pupet too, i mean she is illuminati not me, i just love her music & her vol and her talent as well, so Little Monster, don(t be offended by this, just Don't make a feud
P.S. i'm a little monster too

hur kunk skunk 2 years ago
very good analysis! thumb up!

Genkikaio 3 years ago
@v0rt3x1705 what is with the prayer?

theN4ever 2 years ago in reply to Cesar Alvarez
lets just pretend for a moment that she just artistically put together this video with no agenda. Would any of these images mal sense? No. This video is loaded with symbolism and artists do this because they no people like you won't stop to consider wh you are looking at. Lady Gaga has the theme of transhumanism and occult imagery in most of her videos. God does not advoc this behavior. If Lady Gaga ever talks about God is not the God of the Holy Bible and she will corrupt you.

J koh 3 years ago
i thought it was a PESO sign.. lol

LunaSeaSane 3 years ago
ALSO:

Track tempo: 119 bps.
119 in reverse = 911.
9/11... get it? (There's a transition related occult meaning in these numbers).

Basically, it's starting to sound like a spell.
Show less

Ryanblaaaa 2 years ago
Loool, what aload of old shit.

incredible1210 3 years ago
Very thorough...although it doesn't take a dyslexic this long to read each slide. Hope this didn't take you all month/year to make...

LunaSeaSane 3 years ago in reply to LunaSeaSane
And no doubt in my mind that many, many artists (especially in dance music - hipnotic/distracting/the perfect arena to test these practices) underwent a major faith switch.

clementine amaze 3 years ago
you should state the obvious before you point fingers at the most coincidental things

Madolia Steel 2 years ago
20:19
-Bitches! I AM DRACULA !

Cesar Alvarez 2 years ago
OMG don't you guys have something else to do instead of just saying shit.
Maybe your fucking mom is a witch and your talking about other people
You fucking piece of shit
Leave Mother monster alone
Your just another bully like all of you guys.
F U C K Y O U >=(

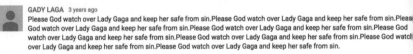

dvdert6 2 years ago
Bad Romance is an ART of Gaga + top of the world directors & public relations = TALK OF THE TOWN. They did this to make the public talk about it more. The more weirder the more people are gonna bite it and spread the word to look at Gaga's video. Why don't you analyze Kesha's Die Young music video. They made the elements clear and repeating to emphasize it so much to get the people to talk about it.

GADY LAGA 3 years ago
Please God watch over Lady Gaga and keep her safe from sin.Please God watch over Lady Gaga and keep her safe from sin.Please God watch over Lady Gaga and keep her safe from sin.Please God watch over Lady Gaga and keep her safe from sin.Please God watch over Lady Gaga and keep her safe from sin.Please God watch over Lady Gaga and keep her safe from sin.Please God watch over Lady Gaga and keep her safe from sin.Please God watch over Lady Gaga and keep her safe from sin.

R.i.C 2 years ago
TWO WORDS BULL SHIT

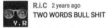

Francesca Coin

Tearing the Neoliberal Subject

Just let yourselves be overthrown!
Nietzsche, Thus Spoke Zarathustra

A few months after the occupation of Gezi Park, Stephen Snyder wrote an article for *Roar Magazine*, in which he described the Turkish protests as a process of transvaluation.[1] Snyder argued that it was a process of transvaluation that had lit up Istanbul, a weaving of dancing and art-making, aesthetic intensities and creative performances. In this weaving, singularity had stripped off its old skin of abstract labor and had spilled over into the streets to celebrate new values. The same scene, after all, is shaking up public spaces the world over, where subjectivity is tearing labor off its back together with its morality, with its interpretations of true and false, right and wrong, good or bad behavior, with a reality that is "false, cruel, contradictory, seductive, without meaning,"[2] as Nietzsche describes it in *The Will to Power*. This process of transvaluation dissolves the old neoliberal era and affirms "an *ascending* evolution of life [...] well-being, power, beauty, self-approval"[3] in a social condition that interrupts the eternal return of the same, that continuous process which since primitive accumulation repeats itself every day by weaving a close tie between morality, capitalist production, and state in order to leave it all behind. In this context that strange encounter through which the individual whose own "capacity for labour, his own person" and "the owner of money meet in the market, and deal with each other as on the basis of equal rights, with this difference alone, that one is buyer, the other seller; both, therefore, equal in the eyes of the law" becomes exotic.[4] The

---

1 Stephen Snyder, "Gezi Park and the Transformative Power of Art," *Roar Magazine* (January 8, 2014), available at: http://roarmag.org/2014/01/nietzsche-gezi-power-art/.
2 Friedrich Nietzsche, *The Will to Power*, trans. Walter Kaufmann and R.J. Hollingdale (New York, N.Y.: Vintage, 1968), chap. 853, p. 451.
3 Friedrich W. Nietzsche, *The Antichrist*, trans. H. L. Mencken (New York, N.Y.: Knopf, 1924), chap. XXIV.
4 Karl Marx, *Capital Volume 1: A Critique of Political Economy*, trans. Ben Fowkes (London: Lawrence & Wishart, 1992), p. 119.

encounter between the owner of money and the owner of labor is suspended here, belittled by the arrogant indifference of one of the two sides. There is a double process in this overflow. To cease being acted upon and acting as abstract labor, the forces reacting against this exchange must reject not only the exchange itself and its value, not only pull out of infinite negotiations on *fair* times and working schedules. This is not merely a case of rejecting the conditions of exchange or of rebelling against the supremacy of the strong over the weak and of the master over the slave. It is rather a question of subverting the values of that exchange.

Something similar happened with the Occupy movement, where the process was easier to observe. The students and precarious workers who attempted to liberate Wall Street were part of the diffused intellectuality born in the last forty years, subject to increasing unemployment and rising levels of debt. For the last twenty years, the US administration has made access to credit subject to continuous mechanisms of evaluation. The transformation of welfare into debt-fare, the dependence on credit to access reproduction, knowledge, housing, or health has imposed on subjects a process of constant evaluation. Through evaluation, capital measures, counts, compares, and classifies every subject in order to reward or punish, separating in this way the deserving from the guilty, the useful individuals from the useless, the best from the rest. In this context merit defines the capacity to constitute oneself on the basis of predetermined expectations, thus demonstrating one's propensity to transform leisure time into working time in order to win in the race to the bottom. In 2011 this process broke down. It was no longer a case of producing the maximum quantity of work at the minimum possible cost. The slogan *lost my job, found an occupation* summed up the happy abandonment of the work ethic and the rejection of the sale of bodies and labor in favor of a communal production of new knowledge and new values.

From this point of view, Marx's *Fragment on Machines* also speaks of a process of transvaluation. A process of transvaluation is what we glimpse when "production based on exchange value breaks down, and the direct, material production process is stripped of the form of penury and antithesis."[5] Then, Marx writes, wealth no longer coincides with the accumulation of money but with the possibility of having time at one's disposal. Work ethic is replaced by the free development of individualities, and hence "not the reduction of necessary labour time so as to posit surplus labour, but rather the general reduction of the

---

5 Karl Marx, *Grundrisse: Foundations of the Critique of Political Economy*, trans. Martin Nicolaus (London: Penguin 1973), p. 705–706.

necessary labour of society to a minimum, which then corresponds to the artistic, scientific etc. development of the individuals in the time set free, and with the means created, for all of them."[6]

This chapter offers a moral reading of Marx, or a materialist reading of Nietzsche. In other words, it looks at the crisis of the law of value through values. Deleuze writes that values look like, or are disguised as, principles: "evaluation presupposes values on the basis of which phenomena are appraised. But, on the other hand and more profoundly, it is values which presuppose evaluations, 'perspectives of appraisal,' from which their own value is derived."[7] If values are disguised as principles, Nietzsche tells us that at the origin of values there is always a hierarchy. At the origin of an evaluation there is always a hierarchy of forces. It is not coincidental, according to Deleuze, that values and evaluation pertain to genealogy. From this point of view, merit—the aspiration to distinction, to cite Nietzsche, the general order of superior moral values through which capital promises to compensate the evaluation of time as utility—always refers to a dialectical order within which capital posits itself as the perspective of appraisal on which the value of all values depends. Throughout the first stage of industrial capitalism the existence of an interpreting subject was hidden in the production of profit: particularly in the West, education and salary were presented as a means of exchange for subsumption, a process that continuously forced the relations of capital and labor to mediation. According to Nietzsche, the willpower expressed by the reacting forces in adapting themselves to a more powerful will is sublime, almost as if the new willpower that appropriates them had in itself the possibility of their reactivation. It may be sublime, but it is still an abortion of the willpower in favor of what is called *responsibility*. In the neoliberal age, this means of exchange no longer exists. Capital has reduced to zero the portion of value exchanged for labor and, as David Harvey puts it, has stopped paying the costs of social reproduction.[8] In this context, the question we may ask is what makes possible and what blocks a process of transvaluation?

---

6 Marx, *Grundrisse*, p. 637.
7 Gilles Deleuze, *Nietzsche and Philosophy*, trans. Hugh Tomlinson (New York, N.Y.: Columbia University Press, 1983), p. 1.
8 Compare David Harvey, *The Enigma of Capital and the Crises of Capitalism* (Oxford: Oxford University Press, 2010).

The Origin of Values

We need to go back to the origin, that is, to the moment when we can observe "the entry of forces [...], the leap from the wings to center stage, each in its youthful strength."[9] By way of the metaphor of the world as a stage, Sandro Mezzadra notes a possible affinity between the Marxian concept of origin (*Ursprung*) and that which Nietzsche defines as emergence (*Entstehung*). We need to return to the origin because that is where we encounter "the protagonists of the drama that forms the historical plot of the capitalist mode of production,"[10] as Mezzadra calls them: active and reactive forces, dominant and dominated, a hierarchy of forces that transforms a long series of processes of oppression in a hierarchy. The origin is always a hierarchy of forces, a process of oppression from which the difference between the forces derives. But as Deleuze wrote, "the origin is the difference in the origin, difference in the origin is *hierarchy*,"[11] the differential relationship from which the value of values is born, that is, the idea of true and false, right and wrong, behind which the stronger will of an interpreting subject is concealed. Following a Marx uncharacteristically dressed up in the garb of a genealogist, we find ourselves back in that timeless zone where the birth of hierarchical relations reveals the origin of all values.

In some ways, Deleuze's reading of Nietzsche allows us to meet another Marx. In the famous chapter 24 of the first book of *Capital*, Marx argues that the primitive accumulation of capital is first and foremost a history of expropriation: It is violence that separates the producer from the means of production. But the history of expropriation that produces dominant and dominated forces, active and reactive forces, owners of capital and the destitute homeless or vagrants, can be traced back to a moral distinction. The dominant forces claim that the hierarchy is the effect of merit and guilt, the way in which God uses money to express a moral judgement on everyone's conduct. In this sense, Deleuze's reading of Nietzsche allows us to re-read capital accumulation in a moral sense, the same process Marx undertakes when he identifies the original sin of political economy in the division between

---

9 Michel Foucault, "Nietzsche, Genealogy, History," in *The Foucault Reader*, ed. Paul Rabinow (New York: Random House, 1984), p. 84.
10 Sandro Mezzadra, "Attualita' della preistoria: per una rilettura del Capitolo 24 del *Capitale*," *UniNomade* 2.0, 16/01/2011, available at http://www.uninomade. org/per-una-rilettura-del-capitolo-24-del-capitale/ (accessed 07/09/2015)—trans. Francesca Coin.
11 Deleuze, *Nietzsche*, p. 8.

dominant and dominated forces: "this primitive accumulation plays in Political Economy about the same part as original sin in theology,"[12] Marx writes. There is no violence, but rather two qualitatively different forces, "one, the diligent, intelligent, and, above all, frugal elite; the other, lazy rascals, spending their substance, and more, in riotous living. [...] And from this original sin dates the poverty of the great majority that, despite all its labour, has up to now nothing to sell but itself, and the wealth of the few that increases constantly although they have long ceased to work."[13]

The origin focuses on a perspective of appraisal where hierarchy becomes a consequence of conduct. The force that imposes obedience "affirms its difference and makes its difference an object of enjoyment,"[14] while the force that is compelled to obey represents something bad, something that must be "rectified, restrained, limited and even denied and suppressed."[15] In this sense, the will to power that establishes itself in the hierarchy as the genealogy of strength and of powers, the qualitative element that determines the difference between forces, also establishes the perspective from which phenomena are valued. The dominant force embodies victory, merit, and excellence, while the dominated forces stand for sin, bad conduct, and guilt in a dialectical relationship that shapes history through the voice of the dominant powers and identifies those powers with the embodiment of progress itself: the avant-garde tasked with separating prehistory from history, antiquity from the future and "a history whose perspective on all that precedes it implies the end of time."[16]

It would be revealing to look at the daily repetition of the process of accumulation from a moral viewpoint starting from the dawn of capitalism, in other words to see in what ways the violence of oppression inscribes itself on the body to define not just the origin of private property but rather the origin of good and evil, of good and bad conduct. Frantz Fanon reflects in depth on the undecidability of truth and falsehood in the colonies, where "the economic infrastructure is also a superstructure. The cause," he writes, "is effect: you are rich because you are white, you are white because you are rich."[17] Colonial power weaves a tight bond with morality, thus subverting the mental coordi-

---

12 Karl Marx, *Capital*, vol. I, chap. 26, p. 507.
13 Ibid, p. 507.
14 Deleuze, *Nietzsche*, p. 56.
15 Ibid, p. 35.
16 Foucault, "Nietzsche," in *The Foucault Reader*, p. 87.
17 Frantz Fanon, *The Wretched of the Earth*, trans Richard Philcox (New York: Grove, 2004), p. xx.

nates of the indigenous population. It celebrates the oppressing powers in immutable intellectual monuments, while the native "can only
recognize with the occupant that 'God is not on his side.'"[18] Behind
beliefs and emotions, behind ways of being, saying, feeling, thinking,
behind the lifestyles produced by their origins, there is always a hierarchy: "modes of existence of those who judge and evaluate, serving
as principles for the values on the basis of which they judge."[19] The
questions we must ask, then, is, what is the origin of values and which
subject is concealed behind the perspective from which we establish
the value of all things?

The Law of Value

Nietzsche and Marx were writing a few years apart, in Germany. At
the time, "modern industry itself was only just emerging from the age
of childhood,"[20] and from three different corners of Europe, Jevons,
Menger, and Walras were each in their way laying the foundations
of economics as an autonomous science, ready to free itself from the
apposition of the *political*—what is usually described as the Jevonsian
revolution of value.[21] From that moment, economic analysis no longer
defined production as a spontaneous innovation of social processes,
but rather as the function of an utilitarian objective, thus opening up
economic discourse to mathematical formalization and to individual-
ism as its methodological foundation. This paved the way for interpreting the birth of political economy as the establishment of a new
perspective of appraisal. It marked a historical turning point: Value is
no longer intrinsic to goods but is expressed as a fraction of a unit of
measurement that is universally applicable.

In the 24 January 1873 postscript to the second edition of *Capital*,
Marx himself gives us arguments for interpreting political economy
as the result of the establishment of a new way of assigning value.

---

18 Frantz Fanon, "Racism and Culture," in: *Toward the African Revolution: Political
Essays*, trans. Haakon Chevalier (New York, N.Y.: Grove, 1994), p. 38.

19 Deleuze, *Nietzsche*, p. 1.

20 Karl Marx, *Capital*, vol. I, Torr ed., p. xxiii.

21 As Ranchetti and Lunghini argue, the revolution of value "rejects the idea that the
value of goods would depend on their intrinsic properties. Such value would on the
contrary depend on the capacity of individual subjects to appraise whether commer-
cial goods might be able to fulfill their needs." Giorgio Lunghini and Fabio Ranchetti,
"Teorie del valore," in *Enciclopedia della Scienze Sociali Treccani* (1998), available at
http://www.treccani.it/enciclopedia/teorie-del-valore_%28Enciclopedia_delle_sci-
enze_sociali%29/ (accessed 07/09/2015).

Economy is not a science, Marx argues. It can only be a science to the
extent that it reflects the values of a specific interpreting subject:

> In so far as Political Economy remains within that horizon, in so far, i.e.,
> as the capitalist regime is looked upon as the absolutely final form of social
> production, instead of as a passing historical phase of its evolution, Political
> Economy can remain a science only so long as the class struggle is latent or
> manifests itself only in isolated and sporadic phenomena.[22]

In fact, what we call science describes the process through which
one particular interpretation asserts itself as a universal way of assigning value. Science is a *symptomatology* and a *semiology*, as Nietzsche
might have put it. It describes a process of capture, appropriation and
management of a portion of reality. We are therefore talking not of science but of a process of oppression within which the more powerful
forces appropriate the name and function of the other forces. In this
instance, too, it is hard not to hear Nietzsche in Marx's words: We are
not talking about science but about a general tendency towards indifference, the ultimate aim of which is "to make up for inequalities,"[23] to
deny differences and to transform life into matter that can be measured
and quantified.

In this context the very concept of abstract labor comes to describe
a symptomatology. It is a mere discourse in signs, as Nietzsche puts it
in "Twilight of the Idols:" "an interpretation of certain phenomena—
more precisely, a misinterpretation."[24] It is not just the concept of
value, then, that needs to be put under scrutiny, but the very meaning of things, the goal they make their own but which they appropriate from the power that captures them. In lieu of life, then, we find
abstract labor whose mathematical representation becomes an anthropological constant that reduces life to something to be measured and
quantified.[25]

From this point of view, the industrial era looks like an exotic anthropological achievement. The concept of value and that of abstract labor

---

22 Marx, *Capital*, p. 11.
23 Deleuze, *Nietzsche*, p. 45.
24 Friedrich W. Nietzsche, "Twilight of the Idols," in: Walter Kaufman, ed., *The Portable Nietzsche*, trans. Walter Kaufman (New York, N.Y.: Viking, 1976), chap. "The 'Improvers' of Humanity," p. 501.
25 "The 'arithmetical presentation' assumes abstract labor: that is, it assumes that labor power as an anthropological constant. Human beings are already exchange-able as different deposits of labor power and thus capitalism is always possible." Jason Raed, "Primitive Accumulation: The Aleatory Foundation of Capitalism," *Rethinking Marxism* 14.2 (Summer 2002), p. 44.

hide a society that is wrenched from the commons and in which the rhythm of monetization increases together with the impossibility of direct access to reproduction. In the first phase of industrial capitalism, "the notion of abstract labor becomes a near natural category, a mere mental abstraction, free from all those characteristics—from mercantile alienation to labor expropriation—that make it a specific category of capitalism."[26] In the introduction to his 1857 *Grundrisse*, Marx describes abstract labor as the starting point of modern political economy and of the very facticity of the producing subject. The question that has long haunted Nietzsche is, why would the subject abdicate its own will to power and form itself on the basis of the will to power of others? Why does a force accept to be appropriated anew for new goals, kidnapped again, and adapted to new finalities?—How does it happen? Nietzsche asks. "'Which one makes it happen'?, you should ask," he retorts. For Nietzsche, the pronoun "which (one)" points to the forces that have taken hold of the meaning of all things: Who is hiding there?[27] In the transformation from what a force "already is" to what it "is not yet,"[28] to cite Pierre Macherey, from *Arbeitskraft* to *Arbeitsvermögen*, from the actual body to the virtual one, as Legrand puts it, another will to power emerges, a will that is more powerful and capable of measuring the other's action in terms of the benefit it can extract from it, a third passive agent that calculates the value of each object in terms of the utility it can bring to itself.

Nietzsche carefully examines this process of appropriation through which the reactive force abdicates its own will to power and forms itself on the basis of extrinsic values. He does not accept this adaptation. He is disgusted by the adaptive will of the reactive forces, he is repelled by it: "Fie on the thought that merely by means of higher wages the essential part of their misery, i.e. their impersonal enslavement, might be removed!" he writes. "Fie, that we should allow ourselves to be convinced that [...] the disgrace of slavery could be changed into a

26 C. Vercellone, „La legge del valore nel passaggio dal capitalismo industriale al nuovo capitalismo," *Uninomade*, available at http://www.uninomade.org/vercellone-legge-valore (accessed 7 December 2013)—trans. Francesca Coin.
27 Nietzsche *Posthumous Fragments*. Deleuze, *Nietzsche*, p. 77; see also translator's note 3*, p. 207.
28 Stéphane Legrand, *Les normes chez Foucault* (Paris: PUF, 2007), cited in Pierre Macherey, "The Productive Subject," trans. Tijana Okić, Patrick King, and Cory Knudson, in: *Viewpoint Magazine*, no. 5 Social Reproduction (October 2015), available at https://viewpointmag.com/2015/10/31/the-productive-subject/.

virtue!"[29] To conclude: "Ah, man returns eternally! The small man returns eternally! [...] Ah, Disgust! Disgust! Disgust!"[30]

Nietzsche traced the abortion of the will to power in everything he examined, from salaried occupation to education, the main target of his critique.[31] The problem for Nietzsche was the slave's desire to become *current*, to circulate, to become a currency. Following Deleuze, one could say the problem is that the slave conceives of power only as "the object of a recognition, the content of a representation, the stake in a competition,"[32] and makes power the result of a struggle the reward of which is the mere allocation of already established values. We are still within a dialectical relationship. To Nietzsche, the slave's shame consists in subordinating nobility to utility, in putting prudence, the calculating intellect, in the place of courage or vital force. Only a slave would replace the reality of his relationships with a perspective that expresses all those relationships in terms of *measure*.[33] Only a slave sells his own will to power for a means of exchange, for money. Only a slave thinks in terms of utility.

"The *aim* now is to preclude pessimistically, once and for all, the prospect of a final discharge," Nietzsche exhorts, "the *aim* now is to make the glance recoil disconsolately from an iron impossibility; the *aim* now is to turn back the concepts 'guilt' and duty [...] against the debtor first of all."[34] For Nietzsche, the slave is precisely he who has for too long looked upon his own natural instincts with *an evil eye*, until those instincts "have finally become inseparable from his 'bad conscience,'" from all "the *unnatural* inclinations [...] to that which runs counter to sense, instinct, nature, animal, in short all ideals hitherto which are one and all hostile to life and ideals that slander the world."[35] The slave makes the perspective of the dominant forces his own: He takes on his guilt, his responsibility, the sacredness of duty, and becomes an animal "with the right to make promises," one that is

---

29 Friedrich W. Nietzsche, *The Dawn of Day*, trans. John McFarland Kennedy (New York, N.Y.: Macmillan, 1911), p. 182.

30 Friedrich W. Nietzsche, *Thus Spoke Zarathustra*, trans. Thomas Common (2010), p. 173.

31 Friedrich W. Nietzsche, *On the Future of Our Educational Institutions*, trans. John McFarland Kennedy (London: Foulis, 1909), p. 36

32 Deleuze, *Nietzsche*, p. 10.

33 Compare ibid, p. 118.

34 Friedrich W. Nietzsche, "On the Genealogy of Morals," in: Walter Kaufman, ed., *On the Genealogy of Morals and Ecce Homo*, trans Walter Kaufmann and R.J. Hollingdale, (New York, N.Y.: Random House, 1989), second essay, section 21, p. 91.

35 Ibid., second essay, section 24, p. 95.

"calculable, regular, necessary,"[36] equal among equals, conforming to the rules and thus predictable.

Nietzsche always saw utilitarianism lurking behind morality. The issue is that the notion of utility refers to a subject capable of interpreting the actions of others as something to be evaluated in terms of the benefit it can draw from them. The framing of utility in Nietzsche's philosophy demonstrates a kind of capture, a more powerful will that separates a force from what is in its power and gives it a name, a use, an aim, a goal. Deleuze points out that morality conceals within itself the utilitarian point of view, such that the qualities morality ascribes— good and bad, good and evil—hide a subject who claims an interest in actions that s/he does not undertake.[37] In this sense, utilitarianism always presupposes a different point of view, a subject that quantifies the actions of others from the point of view of the utility that can be drawn from them.

But looking beneath the surface, Nietzsche reveals an ambivalent attitude towards the abortion of willpower. Deleuze writes that "[t]here is something admirable in the becoming-reactive of forces, admirable and dangerous,"[38] since from a certain point of view in this exchange the reactive forces show what amounts to a will to power. As Deleuze puts it, "reactive force is 1) utilitarian force of adaptation and partial limitation; [...] 3) force separated from what it can do, which denies or turns against itself."[39] "But, in another way, it reveals to me a new capacity, it endows me with a new will that I can make my own, going to the limit of a strange power."[40] This is where Deleuze describes Nietzsche's attitude towards the adaptive process of the reactive forces as ambivalent. The will to power they express in adapting is sublime for Deleuze, almost as if the new power this process gives them was the precondition for a new mode of becoming active, making it possible to cross a new threshold. Power here is not conceived as an object of recognition but gives access to a bigger capability. In this sense, aiming for excellence constitutes the essence of the slave's desire. It refers to that order of superior values to which the reactive force aspires so as to conceal its own wretchedness. Aiming to excel, Nietzsche writes, means desiring to see "our neighbour suffer from us, either internally or externally." It means aspiring to "a long series of stages in this secretly-desired will to subdue," that "marriage of pretences, sophis-

---

36 Ibid., 2.1
37 Compare Deleuze, *Nietzsche*, p. 118.
38 Ibid., p. 66.
39 Ibid., p. 61.
40 Ibid., p. 66.

tication and sickly idealism which is not coincidentally an excellent history of culture."[41] Thus, "pain would be given to others in order that pain might be given to one's self, so that in this way one could triumph over one's self and one's pity to enjoy the extreme voluptuousness of power." Nietzsche almost apologizes for his excitement, for the orgasmic seduction of the will to power, but his research was such that he could not restrain himself, his yearning for that place where the slave finally triumphs "in the vast domain of psychical debaucheries to which one may be led by the desire for power."[42]

Answering the question of what can be found behind the becoming-reactive of the forces appears now much simpler. Behind it we find a world divided between high and low, heaven and hell, good and evil, a world defined by the allegedly superior moral values typical of modern dialectical thought and of Christian ideology, the very world that Georges Bataille mocked when he celebrated his big toe, or the other monuments of the oppressing forces. In this world, those forces embody victory, merit, virtue, excellence, while the oppressed ones are left with sin and guilt for what must be rectified, tamed, repressed. Although such a dialectical relationship might seem pathetic to us, in reality it has long been described not just as a social relation but as a precise direction for human evolution. Without revisiting the debate about the Marxian concept of modernity, it bears mentioning that capital has always used dialectics not just to repress but also to embody the promise of progress, of emancipation, of liberation or of ultimate power. "Capital not only presents itself as measure and as system, it presents itself as *progress*. This definition," Negri argues, "is essential to its internal and external legitimation. [...] Progress is the eternal return lit-up by a flash of a *now-time* (*Jetzt-Zeit*). Administration is illuminated by charisma. The city of the devil is illuminated by grace."[43]

In a sense, we can start thinking about the concept of measure from here. Marx describes the measure of value as the result of an antagonistic relation: the process through which the capitalist, as he puts it, "tries to make the working day as long as possible," while the seller of labor "wishes to reduce the working day to one of definite normal duration."[44] To the subject who sells his labor, the aim is to free up time for "[t]he free development of individualities, and hence [...] the general reduction of the necessary labour of society to a minimum,

---

41 Nietzsche, *The Dawn of Day*, p. 99.

42 Ibid., p. 101.

43 Antonio Negri, *Time for Revolution*, trans. Matteo Mandarini (London: Continuum, 2003), p. 108.

44 Marx, *Capital*, vol. I, part 3, ch. 10, p. 164.

which then corresponds to the artistic, scientific etc. development of the individuals in the time set free, and with the means created, for all of them."[45] For the owner of money, the aim is to capture life for new objectives, to manipulate it anew and use it as a resource to be extracted, but which is inadequate to enjoy the very prosperity it has produced. The measure of value, in other words, must be placed within a context propped up by values, the values defined by the dominant forces. We are faced, then, with a war between antagonistic perspectives of appraisal, each of which proposes a reading of reality that is the opposite of the other's, like an upside-down image.

The Crisis of the Law of Value

As we have seen, throughout the era of industrial capitalism the positive will of the productive forces is directed towards and incorporated into the will of capital through the production of surplus value, which then functions as a means of exchange for the process of subsumption. In this context, liberal democracy and representative governments, particularly in the West, have had a redistributive task, as social struggles and class conflicts reminded them. In practice the negotiation between diverging conflicts of interests was mainly made possible by the disproportions present in the system. The opportunity to extract surplus value rests on disproportion, in particular on the disproportion between surplus labor and necessary labor; surplus value in its turn makes it possible to achieve a temporary agreement between conflicting interests. At the end of the Fordist era the huge increase in the technical and organic composition of capital reduces profits even if the exploitation of labor intensifies, according to Marx. What is slowly revealed is capital as capital, a subject that reaches its full development when it subsumes into itself the conditions of social reproduction. Marx argues that during the crises, capital becomes visible: it is no longer directly involved in the process of production, but it appears "as money existing (relatively) outside of it"[46] The productive forces too are no longer directly involved in that process: free labor,

---

45 Marx, *Grundrisse*, p. 706.
46 "In a general crisis of overproduction the contradiction is not between the different kinds of productive capital, but between industrial and loanable capital— between capital as directly involved in the production process and capital as money existing (relatively) outside of it." Karl Marx, *Grundrisse: Foundations of the Critique of Political Economy*, trans. Martin Nicolaus (London: Penguin 1973), p. 413.

precarious circumstances and unemployment coexist in a relatively autonomous way outside of it.

We are faced with an inversion, or perhaps a separation:

> Beyond a certain point, the development of the powers of production becomes a barrier for capital; hence the capital relation a barrier for the development of the productive powers of labor. [...] This is in every respect the most important law of modern political economy, and the most essential for understanding the most difficult relations. It is the most important law from the historical standpoint. It is a law which, despite its simplicity, has never before been grasped and, even less, consciously articulated.[47]

Beyond a certain point the process of negotiation of value that had defined the industrial era breaks down. Like an upside-down image, the devaluation of labor is reflected in the sparkle of private wealth, while the huge development of the productive forces is reflected in using life itself as a resource to be exploited. What Carlo Vercellone analyzes as the divorce between the logic of value and that of wealth is realized in the formation of two fully developed subjectivities that square up to each other as antagonistic perspectives lying at the margins of the productive process.[48] On the one hand, there is capital in its molar form as the universal creditor and the central management of liquidity. On the other, there is a diffused intellectuality that demands not just the sharing of wealth but an ethical and political rupture with that dialectical world divided between dominant forces and dominated ones, a world against which the movements of the Sixties and Seventies had already fought.

In this context we observe a shift from Marx to Nietzsche, a ninety-degree turn in which conflict is no longer based on the appropriation of value but rather on the assertion of different values. The puzzle for capital is how to reproduce life as a resource to be exploited in spite of the end of scarcity; how to transform leisure time into working time in spite of the fact that productive (not reproductive) labor has become overall superfluous; how to prevent the productive forces from using knowledge to constructive ends. For the productive forces the problem is different. Now that salary is no longer the means of exchange for subsumption; now that the grounds for mediation between capital and

---

47 Karl Marx, *Grundrisse*, p. 748–749.
48 Compare Carlo Vercellone, "La legge del valore nel passaggio dal capitalismo industriale al nuovo capitalismo," available at http://www.uninomade.org/vercel-lone-legge-valore (accessed 7 December 2013).

labor disappear, we must return to the initial question: What makes a process of transvaluation possible, and what prevents it?

Evaluation/Transvaluation

To speak of evaluation or transvaluation we must start from this element: the relative autonomy of money from the productive process. To say that money circulates in a relatively autonomous way from the productive process means recognizing that money functions as the reserve of value and the currency of exchange. This role sends us back to the end of Bretton Woods as a symptom, of the crisis of labor time as a measure of value.[49] Unhooked from goods, money is revealed as the perspective of appraisal of an economic hierarchy at the top of which sit the few financial operators who control global financial flows. As the essence of capital, money takes us to the top of a hierarchy that is situated at the heart of financial markets. It is situated relatively autonomously outside the productive process, as Lazzarato has argued, and functions as a universal creditor or central government of liquidity.[50] Evaluation here means the process through which capital classifies, orders, and compares investment opportunities at the same time as money becomes materialized. The same principle applies to the financing of the public sector, where credit becomes legitimated only insofar as it makes possible an increase in value and return on investments. In the shift from disproportion to crisis, then, neoliberalism becomes the paradigm for restricting access to credit only to those subjects and structures that would be capable of increasing the value of capital's investments. In this context, money becomes the lever through which capital produces the subject and forces it to respond to the needs of the market. This transformation has been particularly intense in institutions of knowledge, as to produce the subject as an assemblage of competencies to satisfy the demands of the market despite the fact that this demand has been increasingly feeble. Here, evaluation fulfills the information function of money: It communicates the value of each sub-

---

49 On this subject, see also Andrea Fumagalli with Stefano Lucarelli and Luca P. Merlino, "Lezioni di teoria della moneta," available at http://economia.unipv.it/pagp/pagine_personali/afuma/didattica/Materiale%20sul%20sito%20del%20corso/Parte%202a%20-%20Teorie%20della%20moneta.pdf
50 This article benefited a great deal from two books by Maurizio Lazzarato, *The Making of the Indebted Man: An Essay on the Neoliberal Condition* (Los Angeles, Calif.: Semiotext(e), 2012) and *Governing by debt* (Los Angeles, Calif.: Semiotext(e), 2015).

ject. Capital ascribes to each subject a numerical value—a rating—on the basis of its place in a list—a ranking—that indicates its ability to excel in a competition of all against all. After demolishing salary as the result of national pay bargaining, the reward system celebrates the winners of this race in which excellence is capital's reward for self-exploitation.

Deleuze writes of *salary according to merit*, a concept which today we might paraphrase as *credit according to merit* as the concept that best encapsulates the difference between the two societies, the disciplinary society and the society of control.[51] Here, merit defines the positive judgement by which capital rewards the subject's ability to constitute itself on the basis of capital's own demands. In general, the concept of merit has been conceived to restore faith in the market at the same time as the fall in profits of the industrial era undermined it. Its task is to be a motivational coach for productivity and for work ethics precisely at the time when working becomes superfluous. But far from bringing a benefit to the producing subject, the concept of merit in effect frustrates it, bringing the subject back into a dialectical position. The elusive essence of the concept of merit disappears whenever a subject is focalized behind it. Once again, we must ask not what but who lies behind the concept of merit, not *what ever,* but *who ever*: What forces have taken ownership of the meaning of this word? Who is hiding within it? Merit is not the weapon for defeating the privilege of the ruling powers. It is the weapon by which the ruling powers absorb the will of others into theirs, thus ensuring that the transformation of disproportion into crisis does not undermine the notion of hierarchy as the natural form of social structure. In this sense merit is the quintessence of hierarchy—it does not free us from it, but reasserts it.

Marx's text "Comments on James Mill" becomes useful here. Marx argues that credit disguises itself as high appreciation for the subject but rewards the individual who "is turned into *money.*" The transubstantiation of flesh into money, the process through which, according to Marx, credit disguises itself as a reward process within which "money is *incorporated* in him"[52] seduces the subject to abort his own willpower and transform himself into the object of capitals desire. It is no longer an abortion in favor of a progressive rationality: it is a mere

---

51 Compare Gilles Deleuze, "Postscript on the Societies of Control," *October* 59 (Winter 1992), p. 3–7.
52 Karl Marx, "Comments on James Mill, *Éléments d'économie politique*," in *Collected Works*, vol. 3, trans. Clemens Dutt, p. 215 (London: Lawrence & Wishart, 1987), p. 215.

capture, a process whereby the subject must produce himself as an object of accumulation

Nietzsche had already observed that the relation of dependence between creditor and debtor allowed the former to inflict on the latter "every kind of indignity and torture [...]; for example, cut from it as much as seemed commensurate with the size of the debt—and everywhere and from early times one had exact evaluations, *legal* evaluations, of the individual limbs and parts of the body from this point of view [...]."[53] The way in which the creditor imposes brutal parameters of evaluation in their tiniest details has not changed until today. What has changed is that there is only one creditor from whose judgement everybody's access to reproduction depends. In an era when productive labor becomes superfluous, the secret for accessing reproduction is to demonstrate its necessity. As if to paraphrase Joan Robinson's provocative 1962 quip that "under capitalism the only thing that is worse than being exploited by capital is not being exploited by capital,"[54] capital transforms access to exploitation into a privilege. In this context, capital

> diminishes labour time in the necessary form so as to increase it in the superfluous form; hence posits the superfluous in growing measure as a condition—question of life or death—for the necessary. On the one side, then, it calls to life all the powers of science and of nature, as of social combination and of social intercourse, in order to make the creation of wealth independent (relatively) of the labour time employed on it. On the other side, it wants to use labour time as the measuring rod for the giant social forces thereby created, and to confine them within the limits required to maintain the already created value as value.[55]

Here, the expropriated can only find redemption in the continuous repayment of an unsustainable debt. As Deleuze and Guattari said, "a time will come when the creditor has not yet lent while the debtor never quits repaying, for repaying is a duty but lending is an option."[56]

53 Nietzsche, "Genealogy," 2.5.
54 Joan Robinson, *Economic Philosophy* (Harmondsworth: Penguin, 1962), p. 46.
55 Marx, *Grundrisse*, p. 706.
56 Gilles Deleuze and Félix Guattari, *Anti-Oedipus: Capitalism and Schizophrenia*, trans. Robert Hurley, Mark Seem and Helen R. Lane (Minneapolis, Minn.: University of Minnesota Press, 1983), pp. 197–98.

Soul-Sourcing

An alien landing on Earth would probably laugh in horror at the way in which some life accepts to compete to the bottom in order to be appreciated by the same subject that has expropriated it. What would jar the eyes of our alien is what is often overlooked by those who study evaluation: the indissoluble relationship between value understood as surplus value expropriated from the producing subject throughout the centuries and evaluation understood as the moral judgment of the expropriating subject towards those who have produced it. In recent years, merit has been interpreted primarily through the Foucauldian category of governmentality, which emphasized the subject's disposition towards fashioning itself as a productive subject. These analyses have opened up an important debate. It seems to me, however, that these analyses sometimes not only risk forgetting the structural causes for the context of crisis in which we are living, but also do not manage to account for the connections between value and evaluation. This means that the key points of the problem are not identified, and neither are the points of rupture, which at times culminates in analyses that have a somewhat conservative aftertaste.

In this context, Lazzarato's critique of the concept of governmentality must be taken seriously. We are no longer in the danger zone where interpretation pushes beyond a point of no return and disappears together with the interpreting subject. Neither is power invisible and omnipresent. Crisis makes capital visible, as Marx argued, even brazen. The discourse of capital, its voice, its attempt to conceal the exploitation by the creditor in the body of the debtor, does not authorize us to forget that capital is a subject. From this point of view, we should take into account the tendency towards *de-governmentalization* practiced by the State and the *de-nationalization* of government. We should recognize behind this tendency a subject capable of directing the conduct of others by using money as a means of blackmail. In other words, we cannot speak of the neoliberal subject without speaking about money, or we will confuse causes with consequences and find capitalism there, in the body, where it does not belong.

I want to step back from Foucauldian interpretations that speak of self-government without coercion. Competition is much more than internalized rationality. It is coercion, blackmail, a matter of life and death. Once more, Nietzsche is useful: The aspiration to excellence is not separable from the ruling hierarchy. The subject who aspires to excel makes others suffer what they would otherwise make him suffer. In other words, the aspiration to excel seems the only way out of a blackmail situation between suffering violence and inflicting it.

It exists exclusively in a dialectical society founded on a Hobbesian rationality of the *mors tua, vita mea* kind. From this point of view, the problem of subjectivity is rather complex. The neoliberal era inscribes the body within a battlefield where antagonistic interpretations are at odds with each other; and the bigger the promise of appreciation, the more intense self-exploitation becomes. As Mark Fisher beautifully argued, the neoliberal era rests on what David Smail called *magical voluntarism*: the belief that it is within every individual's power to make themselves into whatever they want to be. "Magical voluntarism is both an effect and a cause of the currently historically low level of class consciousness. It is the flipside of depression—whose underlying conviction is that we are all uniquely responsible for our own misery and therefore deserve it."[57] Coerced to excel and forced to compete, desire is constantly derailed. Marazzi has neatly defined the process through which capital seems to be able to feed itself on the very flesh of the subject as a form of *crowdsourcing*.[58] His *crowdsourcing* presupposes it seems a kind of *soul-sourcing*, the ability of capital to capture desire and use it to suck its subject back into slavery, an excitement that keeps on sliding towards the quicksand of debt, a process that reveals merit ever more openly as a mystification, a con-trick, a lie.

The Tear

If my argument holds up, then the question is, where does the tear occur? This attempt at a theoretical reframing was meant to arrive precisely here: at the tear. Silvia Federici has often argued that the restructuring of the global economy in the last thirty years has been a response to the establishment of the movements that shook the hierarchies in the Sixties and Seventies. For women, exploitation was then hidden in their bodies. But just as the feminist movement has tried to liberate the body from an interpretation that turned exploitation into the essence of feminine affect, just as the anti-colonial movements have rejected race as the expression of a sort of predisposition towards slavery, the concept of merit locates the responsibility for exploitation in the body and attributes to it the cause of one's own subsumption. To bring capital as a subject back into the analysis serves to free the sub-

---

57 Mark Fisher, "Good for Nothing," online: https://theoccupiedtimes.org/?p = 12841 (available 29 June 2016).
58 Compare Christian Marazzi, *The Violence of Financial Capitalism*, trans. Kristina Lebedeva and Jason Fancis McGimsey (Los Angeles, Calif.: Semiotext(e), 2011), p. 65.

ject from the responsibility that capital would like to hide in the individual. In this sense, to stop the analysis at the reactionary notion of self-fashioning would mean aborting it. On the contrary, the point is to understand where such hiding takes place and where it is ruptured.

Foucault argued that "there is no explanation for the man who revolts. His action is necessarily a tearing that breaks the thread of history and its long chains of reasons so that a man can genuinely give preference to the risk of death over the certitude of having to obey."[59] In "Is It Useless to Revolt?" Foucault looked for the point of rupture. There comes a moment, Albert Camus wrote, when

> [a] slave who has taken orders all his life suddenly decides that he cannot obey some new command. What does he mean by saying "no"? He means, for example, that "this has been going on too long," "up to this point yes, beyond it no," "you are going too far," or, again, "there is a limit beyond which you shall not go."[60]

The slave, according to Camus, affirms the existence of a borderline. Camus's borderline is Foucault's tear: It is the point where the body breaks into the language of capital to speak out the truth. In that instant the body interrupts history and its long chains of reasoning: "But with loss of patience—with impatience—a reaction begins which can extend to everything that he previously accepted, and which is almost always retroactive. The very moment the slave refuses to obey the humiliating orders of his master, he simultaneously rejects the condition of slavery."[61] Here the exchange with the possessor of money is interrupted. The whole point is not to demonstrate that we are worthy of credit; we have already worked enough. It is the creditors' turn to demonstrate their legitimacy.

Translated by Elena Gualtieri

---

59 Michel Foucault, "Is It Useless to Revolt?," trans. James Bernauer, *Philosophy and Social Criticism*, vol. 8, no. 1 (Spring 1981), p. 1.
60 Albert Camus, *The Rebel: An Essay on Man in Revolt*, trans. Anthony Bower (New York, N.Y.: Vintage, 1991).
61 Ibid., p. 11.

Johanna Braun

The American Girl and the Horror of (In)Justice

The justice-seeking dead girl has become an increasingly popular figure in the entertainment industry. The United States in particular is the endemic locus of the epidemic success of the dead girl who seeks justice through revenge. The haunting *girls of justice* can be found as some of the most iconic figures of horror movies, such as the infamous twins in *The Shining* (1980) or the little girl that rushes to the other side to help those who are seeking justice in *Poltergeist* (1982). It is at the turn of the twenty-first century that a range of movies are released in which girls emerge from the dead to call for justice: Little ghost girls whisper their mothers' secrets in *The Sixth Sense* (1999) and *The Others* (1999), the murdered girl from next door reappears in *Stir of Echoes* (1999), the husband's brutally killed underage mistress returns in *What Lies Beneath* (2000), and the out-of-control Samara terrorizes people in *The Ring* (2002).

Recent years have seen a new wave of justice-seeking girls, but those girls—and young women—are (mostly) alive and well and pretend to be haunting presences. Various kinds of cultural output portray this trend, but none more successfully than Hollywood movies such as *Silent House* (2011), *Jessabelle* (2014), *Gone Girl* (2014), and recent productions from young filmmakers, such as *Final Girl* (2015), *Bound to Vengeance* (2015), and *February* (2015). Television series such as *Pretty Little Liars* (2010–), *American Horror Story* (2011–), *Revenge* (2011–2015), *Hemlock Grove* (2013–2015), and *Scream Queens* (2015–) also cover this phenomenon. Several of these productions are adaptions of highly popular books, thus spreading and perpetuating the popularity of those narratives.

They all have one plot element in common: Once an act of injustice is committed against the (predominantly white middle-class) girl, she takes justice into her own hands, even beyond her own death.[1]

However, this figure is nothing new: The girl has always played a crucial role in communicating the errors of the justice system. Since the origin of Justitia—or *Lady Justice*, as she is called in the United States—the *girl in white* has been associated with the democratic system of justice. However, while Lady Justice is always portrayed as a

---

1 Aside from this striking similarity, these productions vary intensely in their motivations and outcome.

calm, righteous judge, the image of the girl has strayed, increasingly conceived of as the victim of an inefficient or corrupt legal system or as an unpredictable slayer. There are many more complex and inter-related reasons for the rise of the justice-seeking girl in popular pro-ductions, but not all aspects can be addressed in this essay. While the vengeful woman is the focus of some insightful studies, the direct link between the girl and the justice system has yet to come to light.[2] In this essay I locate the justice-seeking *un*dead girl in the legal text and draw parallels between legal reality and its fictional doppelgangers. In the beginning I will trace the girl and her very specific legal position in the development of the American legislative text and its impact on fictional narratives of that time. A deconstructive reading of legislative changes from the 1990s to the present will then help us to understand the rise of the vengeful girl in US film and television productions. This essay seeks to understand the rise of the girl in fiction as both symptomatic *of* and in relation *to* the absence or prominence of the girl in the legal text. It is time to recover the girl as a significant historical agent in order to uncover her emblematic singularity.

Let us look closely at whom we are following; *whose footsteps are we tracing?* The justice-seeking girl is a clearly shaped image in a wide range of American literature, film, and television narratives. She is the girl who whispers in the dark, calling your name. She is the noise from under your bed. Her uncanny giggle makes you second-guess your state of mind. She wanders through the house in her innocent-looking uniform, making a spectacle of her appearance. She is the possessed girl, the hysterical girl, or the spectral girl who haunts the family.

---

2 Scholars have thus far paid little attention to the themes of revenge and jus-tice in film and television. While vengeful girls and women are the focus of some iconic studies such as Carol Clover's *Men, Women, and Chain Saws: Gender in the Modern Horror Film* (Princeton, N.J.: Princeton University Press, 1992), Bar-bara Creed's *The Monstrous-Feminine: Film, Feminism, Psychoanalysis* (New York, N.Y.: Routledge, 1993), Jacinda Read's *The New Avengers: Feminism, Femininity and the Rape-Revenge Cycle* (Manchester: Manchester University Press, 2000), and Martha McCaughey and Neal King's *Reel Knockouts: Violent Women in the Movies* (Austin, Tex.: University of Texas Press, 2001), or more recent publications such as Alexandra Heller-Nicholas's *Rape-Revenge Film: A Critical Study* (Jefferson, N.C.: McFarland, 2011), and Claire Henry's *Revisionist Rape-Revenge: Redefining a Film Genre* (New York, N.Y.: Palgrave Macmillan, 2014), the direct link between the girl and the justice system fails to be registered. As evidenced by the titles, the Rape and Revenge genre in particular has received much critical attention for its protagonists and their socio-cultural context. In contrast, it seems the justice-seeking *un*dead girl as an iconic figure (which can be found in a wide range of productions and is now even represented in a prime time soap opera) is widely ignored.

This girl has an agenda; those who are haunted by her must confront her provocation. If she does not receive undivided attention for the cause she represents, she easily loses her temper. Then, nobody is safe from her rage. She can open doors and windows without exertion; she manipulates cutting-edge technology to find entry to your most sacred place. And herein lies the crucial point of her convincibility: *the home.* She will find you in the comfort of your bedroom or stand behind you when you look in the bathroom mirror. She is an expert in discovering your safe haven. Those who are confronted by the justice-seeking girl's rage start asking the burning questions: *Who are you and what happened to you?* As in every courtroom examination, these questions lead to unpleasant answers. We find out that it is not the girl herself who is horrifying, but the things she communicates. After some soul-searching investigations we discover that the horror mediated by the girl does not come from her but from a story, from a historical context. The girl subjectivizes the horror of history, particularly the horror that is produced or concealed by law. *But why the girl? Why is she so prominently attached to the horror of law?* As I will demonstrate, it is her own only loosely defined legal status that enables her to navigate through the hazy corridors of the crumbling house of law.

The Girls' Gothic Home

When we follow the repeating formula of the house, the girl, and the horror of injustice through American narratives, it is quite easy to identify its historical features, to see the resemblance to its ancestor, its Gothic heritage. It was especially in the British Gothic genre of the late eighteenth century in which the image of the justice-seeking girl trapped in a house where all her rights are taken or hidden away from her was professionalized to perfection. It seems as if the American single-family home was built on the foundation of British castle ruins. This begs the question: *Why is the justice-seeking girl so intimately linked to the home?* While the woman was identified with the home, the house's interior, and internal space in general, it is the girl who points to the horror of exactly that home and its connection to the public machinery that stands behind it. The Gothic house as a home to legal operations was a point of reference in fictional narratives as well as the archetype for the haunted house.

The Gothic has a notorious aesthetic, but here I am not concerned with the Gothic as moody and gloomy style. I explore a mode of (hi)storytelling that is specific to the interpretation of the history of law: the *Gothic Mode*.[3] The Gothic Mode is a form of narrating law. Therefore, I emphasize the connections between the Gothic and the law and blend out its aesthetic dimensions, critically scrutinizing Gothic (hi)story as political history. From its inception, the Gothic has incorporated a nationalistic narrative concept rooted in a myth of long-lost ancestors who left an Old World, taking a justice system with them. Sean Silvers identifies this origin in "The Politics of Gothic Historiography, 1660–1800" (2014):

> The "Gothic" did not begin as the kaleidoscopic category it has become. It did not refer to the occult, the macabre, or the supernatural; it was not a genre of horror-driven art, a subgenre of rock music, a style of soaring architecture, or a post-punk subculture with its own recognizable fashion. Nor did it mean, simply, "of or pertaining to the Goths"—the fourth-century civilization in upper Germania—or even, more loosely, "medieval," "antique," or "barbaric." In its original acceptation, the Gothic referred to a partly misremembered, partly manufactured, yet still historically potent myth of origins for the balanced model of English politics.[4]

During the English Civil War (1642–1649) the monarchy glorified an approximately 600-year lineage, as illustrated by the narrative in Nathaniel Bacon's *Historicall Discourse of the Uniformity of the Government of England* (1648), a nostalgic myth of the origin of parliamentarian rule. In this heritage fiction, the immigrant ancestors of the Angles and the Saxons are combined through an arranged marriage. They are not only the so-called "name givers," but cultivate the rhetoric of being "the free people" to their descendants. However, the Gothic ancestors are the source of something more crucial: the heritage of a republican legal system.[5] Another thing the Gothic heritage myth brings to the table is the subjectivization of political origin and law. The liberalism of the American post-1968 student movement and Second Wave Feminist campaigns were therefore in a way already embedded in the oldest layers of the body of law that was English by nature. It comes as no

---

3 For more on the Gothic Mode, see: Alastair Fowler, *Kinds of Literature: An Introduction to the Theory of Genres and Modes* (Oxford: Oxford University Press, 1982), p. 109; and Ruth Bienstock Anolik, "The Missing Mother: The Meanings of Maternal Absence in the Gothic Mode," in: *Modern Language Studies* 33.1/2 (2003), p. 24–43.
4 Sean Silver, "The Politics of Gothic Historiography, 1660–1800," in: Glennis Byron, Dale Townshend, eds., *The Gothic World* (London and New York: Routledge, 2014), p. 3.
5 Nathaniel Bacon, *An Historicall Discourse of the Uniformity of the Government of England* (London: Mathew Walbancke, 1647), p. 96.

surprise that, through this connection of the political and the personal, the space of the individual became a political arena. In his oft-cited *Commentaries on the Laws of England* (1765–1769), the influential legal theorist William Blackstone showed how architecture and politics are tightly intertwined, writing, "Our system of remedial law resembles an old Gothic castle, erected in the days of chivalry, but fitted up for a modern inhabitant."[6] Here it becomes evident that the Gothic castle is not just a governmental building, but a *home*. Around the time when Blackstone published his *Commentaries*, the young Horace Walpole, son of British Prime Minister Robert Walpole, published his influential novel *The Castle of Otranto* (1764). Although Walpole first published the novel anonymously, he later not only acknowledged his authorship but also added a notorious subtitle. *The Castle of Otranto: A Gothic Story* (1765) then introduced to the world a popular method of (hi)storytelling and at once marked the origin of the prolific professionalization of the *Gothic Mode*. In *Otranto*, we find, on the one hand, the castle as the site of a political family drama, and, on the other, the architecture itself, perfectly fitting the legal system Blackstone portrayed. Showing house and home as a hazy structure animated from an unpredictable outside source was thus introduced to the literary canon. In its aftermath, the Gothic offered a range of authors an outlet to comment on contemporary legal questions. Both the house (home) and the legal system are portrayed as *haunted* through this mode of storytelling. British literature at the time—such as Clara Reeve's *The Old English Baron: A Gothic Story* (1778), Sophia Lee's *The Recess, or A Tale of Other Times* (1785), Mary Wollstonecraft's *Mary: A Fiction* (1788), Ann Radcliffe's *The Castles of Athlin and Dunbayne* (1789), and *The Mysteries of Udolpho* (1794) as well as Emily Brontë's *Wuthering Heights* (1847) and Henry James's *The Turn of the Screw* (1898)— also draws heavily on the connection between the home and a defunct legal system.

The early blockbuster Gothic novels and Blackstone's *Commentaries* traveled together to the British colonies and communicated the doctrines of the English Common Law to the colonists. The Gothic Mode not only spread epidemically over the Atlantic, it also spontaneously sprouted branches on its family tree. In order to withstand the ravages of time and obscure its political agenda, the Gothic Mode channeled different narrative forms. From the 1790s to the 1820s, we find a range

---

6   William Blackstone, *Commentaries on the Laws of England*, vol. 4 (Oxford: Clarendon Press, 1765–1769), p. 267–268.

of popular outlets for the Gothic Mode.[7] For example, Sophie Lee's *The Recess* (1783–85) merged the Gothic with the historical novel; Matthew Lewis's *The Monk: A Romance* (1796) introduced the horror genre through the lens of the Gothic Mode; Mary Shelley's *Frankenstein; or, The Modern Prometheus* (1818) initiated science fiction. Decades later, Wilkie Collins's *The Woman in White* (1859) connected the Gothic with the thriller, and Anna Katharine Green's *The Leavenworth Case* (1879) introduced the detective novel to the Gothic. What they all have in common is an obvious interest in the *mechanics of the law*. On both sides of the Atlantic, authors were eager to incorporate this personal and professional interest into their stories. It comes as no surprise then that some of the most influential figures in American and British literature had a background in law: Wilkie Collins completed his legal studies, Henry James went to Harvard Law School, and Charles Brockden Brown worked in a law office before he wrote his novels. Ann Radcliffe's husband had legal training, Horace Walpole's father was an influential politician, and Horace Walpole himself was a member of parliament. Mary Wollstonecraft advocated women's rights and E.D.E.N. Southworth was known for her expertise in Married Women's Property Reform Laws, which she successfully incorporated in her stories. Harriet Beecher Stowe was a staunch abolitionist and human rights activist.

These are only a few figures that highlight the early and direct connection between the rhetoric of law and the Gothic narrative, but they illustrate that the Gothic narrative structure was developed with an expertise in law and law-making. These writers all had a sophisticated understanding of the mechanics of the law and its effect on everyday events. Together they built the American Gothic home as a prime political arena.

The Domestication of the Gothic Castle

While English rule was still housed in the aristocratic castle of the Old World and its ruins, the British colonies transformed these ruins into the now ubiquitous single-family home. Although it took some time to transform the frontier home—the cabin in the woods—into a solid family home, the home as haunted political arena became manifest in the colonies' narratives. The Declaration of Independence solidi-

---

7 See Robert Miles, *Gothic Writing 1750–1820: A Genealogy* (London: Routledge, 1993), p. 1.

fied the identity of the United States, and the unstable cabin in the woods of early Puritan settlements gradually transformed into solid poured foundation homes. But this growth in confidence was still subject to the brutal hauntings of the past. The horror of possession and dispossession (physically and mentally) has been a driving force for both fictionalized and eyewitness accounts of the history of the United States of America. Girls mediate the symbolic horror of oppression: that of indigenous people, of victims of human trafficking and slavery, of women in general. The American girl, turned into a political agent, mediates the gap between defendant and plaintiff. Through this mediation she outs the nation as a polyphonic, cultural hotspot. The girl appears as a disenfranchised entity that calls witness to this horror yet is bound by her involvement in these conflicts.

The former law student Charles Brockden Brown was one of the first to translate the Gothic narrative for a readership in the New World. In his first novel, *Wieland: or, The Transformation: An American* (1798), Brockden Brown plays out the narrative of a utopian home haunted by the Old World Order. While the English Common Law was perceived as a uniting legal structure, United States Common Law varied greatly in its interpretation across the states. The only binding contract all states were and are subjected to is the United States Constitution. This singular uniting document provides that each state is free to build its own law structure under federal constitutional law. Therefore, the individuality of the law was instrumental in the development of the United States' legal structure, which is echoed in the transformation of the monumental aristocratic castle into the suburban single-family home.

In the mid-1800s, Victorian enthusiasm for political conservatism and formidable architectural features resurrected a popular fascination with the Gothic, marking the age of the American Gothic style of single-family domestic architecture. As a perfect stage for public–private dramas in the horror and Gothic genre, the American Gothic home was also voraciously reproduced in both England and its former colonies. One of the main features of Victorian-era architecture is its mutability, which incorporates an amalgamation of different periods and styles. In its late-nineteenth-century iteration, the American home reveals its deep-seated affiliation with the Gothic Mode.[8]

---

8 William Hughes summarizes this phenomenon in his introduction to the *Historical Dictionary of Gothic Literature* (Lanham: Scarecrow, 2013), p. 5.

The Girl in the House of Law

The star of the Gothic narrative is the girl trapped in the endless corridors of an imperfect and oppressive legal system embodied in a haunted home. The girl is the moralistic embodiment of a gaping wound, the failure of the intersection of justice and law. As the symbolic, vehement point of rupture, she is a double negative: a glitch imbued with the power to not only reverse a structural error and seek retribution, but also to allow the corrupt system to implode.

What becomes even more obvious is why the girl who seeks justice is so prominently featured in English and American narratives. The reason may lie in the characteristics of the Common Law, operated through Case Law. Each sentence has the potential to change the law. Therefore, the legal system enables the girl to rewrite history on a case-by-case basis. The legal structure is more susceptible to change than, for example, the Civil Law system, where previous court rulings are only loose guidelines, and the law itself is grounded by comprehensive procedures. Anchoring the narrative of the haunting girl in jurisprudence, however, begs the question: *Why is it the girl who communicates the law?*

The legal status of women and girls in the Common Law of England and its interpretation in the colonies were defined more by women's loss of privileges through marriage than by those which they enjoyed. The legal doctrine of *coverture* in English Common Law had two separate legal statuses for the female population: the *feme sole* and the *feme covert*. Although the term *feme* typically translates to "woman," the word has a connotation that is closer to girl. While the Latin *femina* means woman, *feme* derives etymologically from *femella*, meaning little or young woman. Therefore, the *feme sole* is the singular girl. In contrast to the married *feme covert* (the "covered" girl), the *feme sole* is only mentioned briefly in Blackstone's *Commentaries*. It is precisely her mercurial legal status that enables the single girl to navigate seamlessly through the dangerous territory of the law. Through this loophole, the *feme sole* is able to act as an intact legal person. The girl then becomes the free agent capable of winding through complex pathways to emerge from oppressive social and political structures. It is significant that it is the act of "covering" that renders the girl a woman and wife. This defines the girl not biologically but as a legal status and political position. It is exactly because the girl does not have a clearly defined or strong position in the law that she can operate as the *free agent of justice*.

The girl's overriding goal is to liberate herself from her legal status of the wife or, more specifically, to not run the danger of becoming legally bound. The legal status of *feme covert* brought with it brutal dispos-session. William Blackstone sums it up in his *Commentaries*: "the very being or legal existence of the woman is suspended during marriage, or at least is incorporated and consolidated into that of the husband; under whose wing, protection, and cover, she performs everything."[9] With this legal masking, the husband or legal guardian takes control over every aspect of ownership of his wife. Therefore, it comes as no surprise that husbands—and husbands-to-be—are often portrayed as accomplices to the failed legal structure in the aforementioned narra-tives: masters of the house and aggressive overlords of the girls' prop-erty. This notorious behavior builds their reputation as Gothic villains, some of the most illustrious figures of the Gothic narrative. The Gothic villain professionally rules the machine of injustice and is deceitful in his way of operating the house/home. He is the Gothic girl's nefarious opponent. Although the Gothic villain is such a prominent figure in Gothic storytelling, it is the girl who is so instrumental in communicat-ing and questioning the mechanics of law.

It is significant how girls challenge American legal history and how important it was for them personally (or for their legal assistants) to record their eyewitness accounts. But although we recognize that the girl has always played a crucial role in communicating the errors of the justice system, it is disturbing to see how, especially in the last two decades, the girl has become the horror figure she is today. Since the early twenty-first century, the girl who seeks equity does not sum-mon her victims to trial but drags them to the slaughterhouse. As we will see below, this development has also a progressive side to it. The justice-seeking girl appears in a group of film subgenres that have evolved from the Gothic genre and re-tell the story of the girl trapped in a haunted home that is inhabited by a law-making authority.

A Very Brief History of Justice-Seeking Girls in Film

Since the late 1950s, the evil child, especially the possessed little girl, plays a key role in many horror films.[10] You might know her as Rhoda

---

9 William Blackstone, "Of Husband and Wife," in: *Commentaries on the Laws of England* (Oxford: Clarendon Press, 1765–1769), vol. 1, chap. 15.
10 For more on evil children, see Sabine Büssing, *Aliens in the Home: The Child in Horror Fiction* (Westport: Greenwood Press, 1987); Steven Bruhm, "Nightmare on Sesame Street: or, the Self-Possessed Child," *Gothic Studies* 8.2 (2006), p. 98–113; Margarita Georgieva, *The Gothic Child* (Basingstoke: Palgrave Macmillan, 2013); Adrian Schober, *Possessed Child Narratives in Literature and Film: Contrary States*

in *The Bad Seed* (1956), Karen in *Night of the Living Dead* (1968), or Regan in *The Exorcist* (1973). The girl in close contact with dark, perhaps satanic, alien forces is also the main source of horror in later films such as *Poltergeist* (1982), *The Others* (1999), *The Orphan* (2009), and *Sinister* (2012). What are the socio-political conditions that have turned these once angelic faces so gruesome?

The horrors of displaced property were already evident in early cinema. It is here where the girl, pretending to be a ghost, dresses herself in white sheets in order to protect her property and react to current developments in women's property laws. Films such as *The Haunting of Silas P. Gould* (1915), *Wee Lady Betty* (1917), *The House of Mystery* (1920), *The House of Whispers* (1920), *The Ghost in the Garret* (1921), and *A Fool and His Money* (1925) clearly address the complexity of inheritance laws. These films' protagonists recognize the value of camouflage to protect their property. We find similar scenarios in the Gaslight Film genre of the 1940s.[11] But here it is the husband, the

---

(Basingstoke: Palgrave Macmillan, 2004); Karen J. Renner, *The 'Evil Child' in Literature, Film and Popular Culture* (Abingdon: Routledge, 2013); Sage Leslie-McCarthy, "'I See Dead People': Ghost-Seeing Children as Mediums and Mediators of Communication in Contemporary Horror Cinema," in Debbie Olson and Andrew Scahill, eds., *Lost and Othered Children in Contemporary Cinema* (Lanham: Lexington Press, 2012) p. 1–18; Colette Balmain, "The Enemy Within: The Child as Terrorist in the Contemporary American Horror Film," in Niall Scott, ed., *Monsters and the Monstrous: Myths and Metaphors of Enduring Evil* (Amsterdam: Rodopi, 2007) p. 133–148.

11 The Gaslight Film also gets defined under such terms as *Gothic Romance Film, Paranoid Woman's Film, Gothic Film, Gothic Woman's Film, Female Gothic Cycle, Woman's Melodrama of the 1940s, Gothic Female Melodrama, Female Gothic, Freudian Feminist Melodrama, 1940s Persecuted Women Films, Bluebeard Cycle, Gaslight Genre,* or *Gaslight Melodrama.* See Diana Waldman, "'At Last I Can Tell It to Someone!': Female Point of View and Subjectivity in the Gothic Romance Film of the 1940s," *Cinema Journal*, vol. 23, no. 2 (1984), p. 29–40; Diana Waldman, "Architectural Metaphor in the Gothic Romance Film," *Iris* 12 (1991), p. 55–69; Mary Ann Doane, *The Desire to Desire: The Woman's Film of the 1940s* (Bloomington, Ind.: Indiana University Press, 1987), p. 123–154; Helen Hanson, *Hollywood Heroines: Women in Film Noir and the Female Gothic Film* (London: I. B. Tauris, 2007); Lucy Fisher, "Two-Faced Women: The Double in Woman's Melodrama of the 1940s," *Cinema Journal* 23.1 (1983), p. 24–43; Thomas Elsaesser, "Tales of Sound and Fury: Observations on the Family Melodrama," *Monogram* 4 (1972), p. 2–15 and in: Christine Gledhill, ed., *Home is Where the Heart is: Studies in Melodrama and Women's Film* (London: BFI, 1987), p. 43–69, p. 59; Ian Conrich, "Gothic Film," in: M. Mulvey-Roberts, ed., *The Handbook to Gothic Literature* (New York, N.Y.: New York University Press, 1998), p. 76–81, p. 76; Maria Tatar, *Secrets Beyond the Door: The Story of Bluebeard and His Wives* (Princeton, N.J.: Princeton University Press, 2004) p. 90/92; Tania Modleski, *Loving with a Vengeance: Mass-Produced*

proto-Gothic villain, who tries to steal property from his young wife. Luckily for the wife, she is not his first victim; the former wives of the Gothic villain haunt the house, making the protagonist aware of the Gothic villain's true intentions. It is particularly interesting to consider this against the background of the massive influx of soldiers, alienated from their homes, or returning from the war. After all, it was not just the domestic home that was invaded; the majority of working women lost their jobs as a result of the soldiers' return. Here again, the dispossession of women produces the haunting image of girls. But while the former wives of the Gothic villain had been eager to assist their successor through subtle clues, the tone changed dramatically in the 1960s. Although the narrative is similar, the outcome is quite different. In the next iterations of the Gaslight Film, young women took the place of the Gothic villain. The heiress now had to protect her property from her nieces, daughters, granddaughter, younger cousins, and sisters. We find these new girls in popular movies such as *Bewitched* (1945), *Lizzie* (1957), *Homicidal* (1961), *Dementia 13* (1963), *Hush... Hush, Sweet Charlotte* (1964), *Picture Mommy Dead* (1966), *The Ghastly Ones* (1968) and *What's the Matter with Helen?* (1971). In blockbuster films like *The Innocents* (1961) and *The Haunting* (1963)—which resurrect the domestic manor, symbolic of the Old World Order, as the familial domain—it is now the protagonist who is the source of horror. Here we find girls who are pathologically perilous, capable of psychotic breaks in an effort to secure their control over the American home. Even when the events have an implied supernatural origin, it is almost exclusively a mad girl who runs the show.

The twist is that while the haunted and haunting housewives of the original films were legally hidden because of their status as *feme covert*, the younger generation operates exclusively from the position of *feme sole*. While the image of the devoted housewife and mother was still propagated through celebrities like June Cleaver, one increasingly found the girl in the position of dissent. It is no coincidence that Lesley Gore's hit song "You Don't Own Me," Betty Friedan's influential *The Feminine Mystique*, and the signing into law of the Equal Pay Act all collided in 1963. Yet, the girl who protested for and demanded expanded women's rights was rendered on the screen as a violent home intruder. Habitually, those girls are brutally punished in the course in many horror films of the 1960s and 1970s and can

---

Fantasies for Women (Hamden, Conn.: Archon Books, 1982), p. 21; Guy Barefoot, *Gaslight Melodrama: From Victorian London to 1940s Hollywood* (New York, N.Y.: Continuum, 2001).

be seen in direct correlation to the Slasher Film genre. The Slasher Film from the 1970s introduces the concept of the *final girl*, a term coined by Carol Clover in her groundbreaking analysis, *Men, Women, and Chainsaws* (1992). While the final girl is mostly an innocent girl that has to become resilient and resourceful in order to survive, the Gothic villain is instrumental in her ordeal. In contrast to the oppressive husbands in Gothic literature and the Gaslight genre, here the Gothic villain becomes a grotesque creature, a monster of preposterous proportions. The Gothic villain is now a cruel rapist and child molester. In films such as *Black Christmas* (1974), *Texas Chain Saw Massacre* (1974), *Halloween* (1978), and *Nightmare on Elm Street* (1984), girls are violently hunted down by villainous men and boys.

What becomes evident in these examples is that, while the girl was instrumental in negotiating women's rights in those narratives, her own rights were still nebulous. This changed drastically in the early 1980s when the girl started to negotiate on her own behalf.

At the end of the twentieth century something strikingly happened: The justice-seeking girl arises in fact and fiction as a law-making authority. The identity of the girl and the cause for her cries for justice converge with great intensity. Now it seems nearly impossible to differentiate one from the other. In this sense the girl is not only objectively fighting for a cause, but the cause becomes her mission. The girl becomes the subjectivity of justice: the subject of law. To get a better understanding of this development we must take a closer look at legislative changes from the 1990s to the present.

The Dead Girl in the Legal Text

The 1980s and 1990s witnessed an extensive revision of the United States justice system. A group of missing or murdered girls were instrumental in changing the legal debate. Here the dead girl arises as the agent of justice, in whose name the family or community campaigns for drastic changes in the justice system.

The murder of Polly Klaas was instrumental in the enforcement of the *Habitual Offender Laws*, or the so-called *Three Strikes Laws*. After the twelve-year-old was abducted from her bedroom during a sleepover party in 1993 to be raped and murdered, those legislations introduced harsher prosecutions for repeating offenders. A year later, the *Jacob Wetterling Crimes Against Children and Sexually Violent Offender Registration Act* was introduced as part of the *Federal Violent Crime Control* and *Law Enforcement Act of 1994* (which contains the additional *Violence Against Women Act*). In the aftermath, each individual state was asked to create a sex offender registry. In 1996, the *Wetterling Act* was extended by *Megan's Law*, which allows the public not only to view these registries, but also to receive an official notification once a convicted sex offender moves into their neighborhood. *Megan's Law* is named after seven-year-old Megan Kanka in New Jersey, who was brutally raped and murdered by her neighbor in 1994. *Megan's Law* enabled the often criticized public visualization of sex offenders.

Polly Klaas's family collaborated with other affected families to reinforce their campaign for improvements in the legal system. In the case of the kidnapping and murder of nine-year-old Amber Hagerman in 1996, who is still missing, her family actively campaigned for tighter controls and measurements for sexual offenders. At the insistence of Polly's father, Marc Klaas, and with the support of congressman Martin Frost, the *Amber Hagerman Child Protection Act* was introduced in 1996. This law introduced a national sexual offender database and alert system. The *America's Missing: Broadcasting Emergency Response*, or *AMBER Alert* in short—which was widely covered in the media—was introduced in the same year. This notification system alerts neighborhoods and communities immediately when a child goes missing. While the *Amber Hagerman Child Protection Act* only applied to under-16-year-olds, the age group for the alert system was extended after the case of 19-year-old Suzanne Lyall. Suzanne Lyall vanished without a trace in 1998 and remains missing. *Suzanne's Law* was introduced in her name in 2003 to alert law enforcement officers immediately when a child or teenager goes missing and not to wait until 48 hours have passed, as in the case of missing adults. News of the missing teenager is sent directly to the *National Crime Information Center* (NCIC) at the Department of Justice in order to initiate interstate search operations.

The *Jessica Lunsford Act*, or *Jessica's Law*, named after nine-year-old Jessica Marie Lunsford, who was abducted, abused, and murdered by a convicted sex offender in Florida, followed in 2005. Prominent media coverage of the case portrayed sex offenders as lifelong threats. Thanks to *Jessica's Law*, sex offenders are now electronically monitored to prevent them from becoming chronic criminals. In May 2014, *Megan's Law* was expanded by an international notification system, which meant that US authorities release information on the whereabouts of registered sex offenders on an international level.

In 2009 *Kelsey's Law* was introduced, named after the kidnapped, raped, and murdered 18-year-old Kelsey Ann Smith. After Smith was abducted in broad daylight from a store in Kansas in 2007, it took authorities four days to locate her body. The cellphone company Verizon was unable to release the necessary information on the cell phone's location to local law enforcement. *Kelsey's Law* allows law enforcement to gain access to cell phone data and locate the device in an emergency.

Finally, in 2008, various victims' rights were bundled in the *California Victims' Bill of Rights Act*, or short *Marsy's Law*. *Marsy's Law*, named after Marsy Nicholas, who was stalked and murdered by her ex-boyfriend in 1983, is a Californian State Constitutional Amendment. It expands the legal rights of crime victims, increased criminal offenders' restitution, restricting the early release of inmates, and changed procedures for granting and revoking parole. In 2015, it became a law in Illinois.

Chelsea's Law, named after raped and strangled 17-year-old Chelsea King, was signed into California State Law in 2010. *Chelsea's Law* allows life without parole sentences and lifetime parole with GPS tracking for first-time as well as repeating adult child molesters.

Megan's Law, Jessica's Law, Suzanne's Law, Kelsey's Law, Marsy's Law, Chelsea's Law, and the *AMBER Alert* enable girls to bring justice from the dead. Those court decisions noticeably collide with a group of film productions where *un*dead girls arise as brutal agents of justice.

In the form of the ghost girl, the wronged dead girl attacks the tranquility of the utopian single-family home. This violent little home-wrecker becomes the starlet of the entertainment industry at the turn of the century. In movies such as *The Sixth Sense* (1999), *The Others* (1999), *Stir of Echoes* (1999), *What Lies Beneath* (2000), *The Grudge* (2004), *Dark Water* (2005), *Shutter* (2008), *Jessabelle* (2014), and the immensely popular film series *The Ring* (2002–2017) we find ghost girls who persistently haunt family life until their cases are satisfyingly solved. In recent years we have even seen the undead girl in a wide range of television productions: girls who pretend to be of supernatural origin—as in *Pretty Little Liars* (2010–)—or who brutally haunt those responsible, under false identities—as in *Revenge* (2011–2015) or *Scream Queens* (2015–). Supposedly supernatural events are firmly grounded in reality, a tendency which is also included in several film productions, such as *The Uninvited* (2012), *Silent House* (2012), *Final Girl* (2015), and *February* (2015).

These examples imply that the girl is not only responsible for making law and order, but that the justice-seeking *un*dead girl is produced by an inefficient law and that it is therefore her purpose to correct this glitch. The justice-seeking girl arises as the (factual and fictional) popular all-American girl through whom legal debates are visualized. A deconstructive reading of the legal texts in relation to their fictional doppelgangers has revealed that the girl has not only negotiated legal proceedings, but emerges—particularly in recent years—as a law-making authority herself. While these factual and fictional narratives have consistently accorded the girl a legal force that has the power to call the legal system into question, finally at the beginning of the twenty-first century, she rewrites the law.

The girl starts to excessively enforce her own rules, and she is uncompromising and unpredictable in her verdicts. Furthermore, her unpredictability reveals her affiliation with the symbolic order of the law and its mechanics.

The girl takes control of the narrative and takes justice into her own hands. The girl writes her own laws, or they might be produced, implemented, and enforced in her name, revealing once again how the girl herself is already inscribed in the law. She is located in the midst of the legal system and overwrites it from the inside. The girl is solidified in her symbolic severity. Thus, the original concept of the Gothic villain is transferred to the girl. The girl overthrows the ruling power structures of the Gothic villain and drags him from his throne. She is no longer compelled to navigate through the haunted house itself. She now operates the American Gothic home, and in this house there exists only one rule: the law of the girl, the girl's law.

Angela Melitopoulos

Autism and Networks[1]

Teacher, therapist, author, filmmaker, philosopher, and poet Fernand Deligny left behind a multifaceted body of work, documented in an almost 2,000-page book edited by Sandra Álvarez de Toledo in 2007. Designed with care, *Fernand Deligny Œuvres* is a comprehensive volume which traces the networks of Deligny's encounters and collaborations through its many articles, maps, journals, novels, drawings, and film stills. It extends the classical understanding of individual authorship to *many* by making use of everything "that came in range, the closest as well as the farthest away,"[2] but could not be named, as Gilles Deleuze and Félix Guattari remark at the beginning of *A Thousand Plateaus*.

Deleuze and Guattari kept their names as authors of *A Thousand Plateaus* "out of habit," in part to make themselves *unrecognizable* and to *render imperceptible* what makes them "act, feel, and think."[3] The fact that Deligny is only rarely mentioned at the beginning of *A Thousand Plateaus* as an important inspiration and fundamental influence for the concept of the *rhizome* is therefore quite crucial. The citing of names would hinder the reader from understanding what makes the authors "act, feel, and think" and make the "I" identifiable in a given order, which rips the statement out of a murmur.[4] The non-naming of names places emphasis on the multitude of motivations and matters. Deligny thus remains one of these marginally named in order to let the subject–object relations in *A Thousand Plateaus* play out in the background. Taking into account the Research Group Deligny along with Deligny himself, the number of people who go unnamed in the original French edition of *A Thousand Plateaus* increases substantially.[5]

In the 1970s, according to Sandra Álvarez de Toledo, autistic children and researchers of psychotherapy visited Deligny's therapeutic

---

1   This is a revised excerpt from Angela Melitopoulos's Ph.D. thesis, "Machinic Animism and the Revolutionary Practice of Geo-Psychiatry."

2   Gilles Deleuze and Félix Guattari, *A Thousand Plateaus: Capitalism and Schizophrenia*, trans. Brian Massumi (Minneapolis, Minn.: University of Minnesota Press), p. 3.

3   Ibid.

4   Ibid.

5   I use the term Research Group Deligny or Organism Deligny for the fluctuating group of people who worked with Deligny.

network in the Cévennes every summer to take a "vacation from everything that is language, consciousness, and unconsciousness"[6] and to
take part in daily life with Deligny and his group. The *many* were a
fluctuating, heterogeneous group of workers, therapists, artists, filmmakers, students, political activists, and other unnamed persons who
gravitated to this very real research location over decades, where they
lived, studied, and made films together and with autistic children.
Their relation to the location and to the group emerged continuously
as an interface between cartography, writing, photography, film, and
publication, and, most importantly, the famous *Wander Lines* drawings (French *lignes d'erre*) of the movements of autistic children in
their environment.

The political force-field of an open, experimental milieu, in which
the *many* implied in the Research Group Deligny are personified by
Deligny's name, begins with the political act of an inquiry which wants
to explore the existential field between the verbal and the non-verbal.
Young people with autism and non-autists alike formed part of an
organism whose operative functions were too numerous to list in the
credits of the films compiled in *Le Cinéma de Fernand Deligny.*[7] Fernand Deligny's poetic talent yielded the crystallization of a multi-modal
artistic-therapeutic practice into a rhizome-like interface that became
the nodal point of a cinematic practice. Although the DVD's title might
suggest otherwise, the cinema of Fernand Deligny is not auteur cinema
but rather a cinema movement. The films *Le Moindre Geste* and *Ce
Gamin, là* were two of cinéma verité's most important collective documentary and essay film projects. These films were not well-planned
endeavors but rather the effort of an organization to engage in more
radical, process-based, cinematic-psychiatric research with neuro-
diverse young people. They were experimental setups, scientific labo-
ratories, scholarly life studies situated in the open space. A 16mm film
camera was part of the production process, actively structuring the life
and research practices. The collective praxis in this therapeutic center
for research with neuro-diverse youths was meticulously documented
over many years. The film documentation itself became part of the
social milieu's observation apparatus.

Deligny referred to his collaborators as *guardians and educators*
(*gardiens et éducateurs*). Like the Catalan psychiatrist and founder of
institutional psychotherapy François Tosquelles, Deligny made it a pri-

---

6 Fernand Deligny, "La tentative," in: *Fernand Deligny Œuvres*, ed. Sandra Alvarez
de Toledo (Paris: L'Arachnéen, 2007), p. 692—trans. AM.
7 Fernand Deligny, *Le cinéma de Fernand Deligny* (Paris: Éditions Montparnasse,
2007) [on DVD].

ority to work with non-professional therapists, autodidacts, and self-taught people in this therapeutic milieu. They became part of an *existential territory* that was characterized not by words but by gestures. The group worked, sketched, and documented in order to interpret the traces of a new experimental praxis in which Deligny hoped to dissolve the intersubjective order that reigned supreme in psychiatry at the time. "What is the goal of our practice?" he wrote to Louis Althusser in 1976, "This or that 'psychotic' subject? It is certainly not a real object which is to be transformed, but rather it is us, we who are here, we who are close to these 'subjects,' who, quite frankly, are hardly subjects in the common sense, which is exactly why they are here."[8]

Deligny engaged in the daily practice of *tracing* in the Research Group Deligny—a praxis of drawing, filmmaking, writing poetry, and researching that was modeled neither on La Borde and its debate clubs nor on art therapy. The core group who lived the everyday life in this nonverbal milieu fought together with Deligny against a world based on verbal communication, language, and enunciation. They were connected to a "destiny that was bound to a lost cause: that of silence."[9] The first and best-known sketch of the *Wander Lines* was made in 1967 by Deligny's faithful collaborator, Jacques Lin, a former Hispano-Suiza car factory worker who had long traded in his factory work for a life in *institutional psychotherapy* at La Borde. He was one of the main figures in Deligny's research group. At Deligny's suggestion, Lin sketched the maps of the pathways of Janmarie, a young autistic person at La Borde, before departing in order to deal with "his fear and feelings of powerlessness in the face of the violent behavior of the autistic children."[10] Lin began to map Janmarie's walks in the landscape and thus to overcome his own powerlessness and speechlessness. He was meticulous in the process; it was his precise and studious hands that initiated the series of the *Wander Lines* maps that would later fundamentally advance the concept of the *rhizome* and the notion of territory as a form of expression as it was later conceptualized in "The Refrain" in *A Thousand Plateaus*. It is through a praxis of tracing that the *Wander Lines* visualized points of reference in a landscape that became a fluctuating cosmos that one might feel alienated from or unconnected to if no artistic tools for tracing were available.

---

8 Fernand Deligny, "Lettre à Louis Althusser," *Fernand Deligny Œuvres*, p. 24—trans. AM.

9 Fernand Deligny, "Ce silence-là ou le mythe du radeau," *Fernand Deligny Œuvres*, p. 694—trans. AM.

10 Ibid.

Deligny proposed a method of mapping using operative lines that relate itineration to meaning and create a porous virtual space of an *existential territory*. Deligny's handwritten notes can be found on the margins of the famous drawings and cartographies of the *Wander Lines*. In the film *Ce Gamin, là*, he explains how the arrangement on the map puts the reader's eye in search mode—moving between text and map. In the film, his explanation of this relationship is conveyed by a montage of images, starting with the drawing, transitioning to the map and then to film sequences showing the autistic Janmarie in the landscape. The observer's gaze follows Janmarie's itineration, the eye wanders, and the mind is invited into mysterious doings, which is characteristic of Deligny's research: the tracing, drawing, or *whizzing* that Deligny calls the "proper (ontological) realm of the human" in his and Guattari's publishing project *Les Cahiers de l'Immuable*.

> Here, in the *Cahiers*, we focus on the fact that tracing is what is peculiar to humans, who have the power of words that make them in into what they are. That is why we have invented these maps for ourselves. Transcribed with pencils, the traces of our trajectories and our familiar gestures appear. The lines of our wanderings are inscribed with Chinese ink in the trajectories of that which happens to a non-speaking child who is engaged in our things and our way of doing things.[11]

Tracing embodies the essence of action itself. Tracing is not a representation of space but rather a translation of gestures by gestures. It longs for a trans-modal activity that shifts between different modes of perception, that lets us drift from words to our bodily gestures, to our hands that sketch a face, for example. The film *Ce Gamin, là* purposely shifts the spectator's eyes from the dynamic expression of Janmarie's face to the surface structure of the film material itself: the high-contrast, consumed decay of the black-and-white 16mm film frame. This wandering, drifting around, fleeting, and halting of our gaze between text, image, voice, and trace, leads us to observe the entire texture without giving preference to any of these structural moments, which, according to Deligny, fundamentally fill and determine our being.

Here tracing is not simply a reproduction of one's view of a geographical landscape on paper; that is to say, tracing is not just a reproductive act that expresses a process of perception. It is also not only a submission to the normative form of reading or the learned perception of a landscape, as Deleuze and Guattari implied in their argument dis-

---

11 Fernand Deligny, "Revue Recherche, Cahiers de l'Immuable," in: *Fernand Deligny Œuvres*, p. 811—trans. AM.

tinguishing between the reproductive drawing and the operative map. (Deleuze and Guattari themselves questioned this argument because of its binary logic that divides the argument into the good map and the bad drawing.) "The rhizome is altogether different, a map and not a tracing. [...] What distinguishes the map from the tracing is that it is entirely oriented towards an experimentation in contact with the real."[12]

This differentiation evidences a lack of experience in the practice of drawing as tracing itself, as it refers only to the sketched traces of the drawing as representation but not to the intellectual effort of tracing that is part of the practice of drawing, in which one's memory must perform complex operations and is thus operative and non-representative as well.

The Research Group Deligny turned the aesthetic, institutional, and micro-political milieu of *institutional psychotherapy* into an operative space of action for a nonverbal mode of perception by way of thinking and living a mental resistance to the hierarchical structure of language in therapeutic frameworks. Deligny's visual practice follows the lines of flight of vision itself.

The maps of the autistic youths' *Wander Lines* describe the fleeting movement of our perception as a nomadic mode inherent in it. Leaving the question of autism behind, the artist, poet, and therapist Deligny analyzed what the seemingly aimlessly drifting gaze of the neuro-diverse could mean. This gaze, which "is homeless in vision" and "which sees things as they are" before they are obscured by language, describes the movement of passing, of multiple, reticular relationships that we can only register by setting ourselves in motion or by tracing movement rather than space. For Deligny, this non-obscured vision, which can be interpreted as a motivation of artistic research in general, comes from the "prehistoric" age of language, where *prehistoric age* should not be confused with the beginning of time but rather designates a time when language had not yet come into existence. Non-obscured vision is always virtually present and releases the potentiality of a body that is common to all, a "body that is not yet one or the other."[13] This body is a solitary body of perception that allows for the psycho-political alliance of becoming-animal, for example, which is positioned as an act of resistance against the normative, oedipal family triangle in *A Thousand Plateaus*.

---

12   Deleuze and Guattari, *A Thousand Plateaus*, p. 12.
13   Fernand Deligny, "Ce silence là *ou* le mythe du radeau," in: *Fernand Deligny Œuvres*, p. 699—trans. AM.

The form of this alliance appears in Deligny's *Journal d'un educateur* (1965) as a momentary glimpse in the hail of bombs of the Second World War. He begins his recollection of the bombardment of France in 1941—which he experienced as a therapist and teacher for children with intellectual disabilities in the Armentières psychiatric clinic in Nord-Pas-de-Calais[14]—with short pictorial sequences:

> We are five in a truck, the sky is blue. There are airplanes overhead and they are as big as pinheads, diamond pins that launch thin swords of light. Our eyes, being forced to watch, are tearful. We are being bombed. We take cover along a wall to protect ourselves. There is a road on the other side of this little wall, where bags of flour are densely packed, almost hard. Whatever happens in the sky I can do nothing about.[15]

One of the flour bags was ripped open, looking like the white crater of a volcano. Nestled at the bottom of this crater were six gray mice as big as "fingertips. They sleep in a small heap, overfed, full of sun, of milk, of life."[16] In this moment when Deligny no longer had any determining power over his own life, he crouched over the bag of flour and watched the little creatures, feeling close to them.

> Their heart beats and me, I am closer to them […] than to my father, who was killed in 1917 at the Biette farm, closer to these six mice than to anyone, because they live so far away from the event that they cannot be touched by it. While, in the depths of myself, I am just as innocent, just as foreign, just as little human as possible, my life is the very life of these little creatures, but I have a uniform. I'm there beside the river and I do not care as much as the rest; quite as indifferent to geography as to history—out of time and space. Idiot. The wars of today do not respect "idiots." They respect nothing, neither idiots nor the insane.[17]

This passage's sequence of images confronts the reader with a detailed framing that makes clear how strong Deligny's alliance was with this innocent nest of mice. His becoming-animal is based on his solidarity with the little creatures, who, innocent like himself, are exposed to the

---

14   Nord-Pas-de-Calais is an administrative region of France. It was bombarded and occupied by the Germans in 1940, at the same time as Belgium and the Netherlands.
15   Fernand Deligny, "Journal d'un educateur," in: *Fernand Deligny Œuvres*, pp. 12–14—trans. AM.
16   Ibid.
17   Ibid.

violence of war. The inevitability of the impending bombardment led Deligny to think, in his hastily found cover next to a street wall, that nothing about his destiny's present circumstances can be changed, no matter what "is going to happen up there in the sky." This moment of inevitability in the force field of the possible remained forever an important level of perception for him. He later named the series of texts from this period *Les Cahiers de l'Immuable*. For Deligny, the inevitable is the central condition of the reality in which we operate.

During the war, he experienced the killing of people with disabilities as a part of everyday life at the psychiatric clinic in Armentières. The following lines in his journal, which he wrote in 1966, let me assume that he associated the image of the small gray beings (the gray mice) with the image of children with whom he worked during the war and who were killed in the war.

> Six of them have just been killed under the rubble of Pavilion 9 in the vast asylum where I work. Even though they had their gray velvet uniforms, the gray velvet of this asylum, there are more than a thousand here to wear. So these morons die because of a war—they who did nothing to cause it...[18]

His motivation to engage years later in a *politics of experimentation* in *institutional psychotherapy* and in radical research methods on the potentials of non-verbal communication becomes quite evident. It served to protect him against the normative violence of society, and strengthened solidarity in this struggle with Guattari and Tosquelles.

Sandra Álvares de Toledo describes Deligny as someone who spent his entire life in the institutional asylum system and who after the war created a therapeutic research center for mentally disabled children and autistic individuals in the Cévennes as a kind of inner exile for himself. The asylum became "his island, the birthplace of a second, definitive condition of exile, that of writing."[19] The asylum was a protective space for him when confronted with the offending forces of cultural technology and their processes of production. In his studio in the asylum he inhabited a kind of scriptorium within which he developed his poetic, philosophical language. Like Guattari and Jean Oury at La Borde, and like Tosquelles at Saint-Alban, he created an environment within which the forces at work could continuously re-articulate themselves and where these articulations could subsequently be reintegrated into the organization of the therapeutic milieu.

---

18 Ibid.
19 Fernand Deligny, "Nous et l'innocent," *Fernand Deligny Œuvres*, p. 691—trans. AM.

What constitutes the shared basis of existence and communication of the autistic children and the Research Group Deligny? The prehistoric or prelinguistic is virtually anchored as an unexplainable foundation in the present. Deligny claims that we do not sense the specific temporalities of neuro-diverse perceptions that exist as primeval realities not yet obstructed by culture but appear through a virtual plane as an open field of potentiality between autistic and non-autistic people.

In the film *Ce Gamin, là* he says about Janmarie, who is seen crouching on the bank of a brook, playing with the water surface, "And how to know what he is hearing? Which voices that have sound and yet speak of a time when none of the human beings was discriminated against by language?"[20] Through the film this diversity of the perception of time that potentially connects in a virtual plane became the subject of the Research Group Deligny's cinematic explorations. That which was once just a stone could figure as an object in a future action, or what listening to murmuring water means to neuro-diverse people can become part of a shared virtual space. Deligny comments on Janmaries action in the film,

> Once upon a time there were men and stones. They stayed near the springs, and they didn't know why. Water is not used up by drinking. And the stones are here as well … We can sit on them, crack nuts on them, build walls with them, use them as road markers, without depleting their supply.[21]

His commentary on Janmarie's gestures in the film reflects the multiple uses of an object exemplified in a stone that becomes a tool, or a potential chair; as something that can trigger various actions, a virtual possibility from a prehistoric past which Deligny understands as a time in which the functions of possible/virtual actions are "not used up." In the film, an object in the form of a clay dice that Janmarie rolls on a stone becomes the magical key that dissolves the barriers of non-communication between the autistic children and the Research Group and turns the object into a coded sign through which the Research Group's common space of action was shared.

Tracing and mapping for Deligny are, first and foremost, means by which to surpass the limits of a political reality of exclusion in order to dissolve the normative distinction between neuro-typical and neuro-atypical bodies.

---

20 Fernand Deligny in *Ce Gamin, là*, dir. by Renaud Victor and Fernand Deligny (1975). See Annex 2: *Assemblages* by Angela Melitopoulos and Maurizio Lazzarato (2009).
21 Fernand Deligny in *Ce Gamin, là*, see Annex 2.

Philosophers Erin Manning and Brian Massumi posit in their research on the neural-atypical capacities of autistic individuals that autism has the capacity to "bestow equal attention to the complex textures of the entire sphere of life," and to attain an "enchanted and non-hierarchical commitment to method" often similar to that in art, "in which organic and non-organic, colour, smell and rhythm, perception and emotion" are intensively interwoven "with the surroundings of a structured world" that "comes alive through its differences."[22]

Le Moindre Geste and the Ciné-Eye of Josée Manenti

In the early 1960s, years before the film *Ce Gamin, là*, there was the film project *Le Moindre Geste*, which preceded and prepared the project of mapping and tracing. It was realized by a different group of people around Deligny. *Le Moindre Geste* is one of the most impressive film essays of 1960s French cinema, was shown at the 1971 Cannes Film Festival, and made Deligny's work well-known in France. Beyond the exceptional aesthetics of the narrative, the film presents us with surreal narration of a landscape and scenery that has freed itself from the conventions and mechanisms of professional film production. "That which is realer than reality"—to quote Tosquelles—makes *Le Moindre Geste* both an achievement in the arts as well as a scientific and philosophical document.

The film's production lasted from 1961 to 1971, although technically it began in 1958, when Deligny and François Truffaut met to work on the screenplay for *Les 400 Coups*. In order to finance his research for *Le Moindre Geste*, Deligny hoped to win over Truffaut. He insisted, however, on not turning the juvenile delinquent into the symbolic cinematic figure of a societal outsider. Instead, he wanted to film the communal life of ten crazy people who would retreat to the Cévennes in order to live there like in paradise, "like before the first sin or after the final judgement."[23]

---

22   Ralph Savarese, quoted in Erin Manning and Brian Massumi, "Coming Alive in a World of Texture," *Dance, Politics & Co-Immunity: Current Perspectives on Politics and Communities in the Arts Vol. 1*, ed. Stefan Hölscher and Gerald Siegmund (Berlin: Diaphanes, 2013), pp. 73–96. See also Ralph Savarese on the concept of "aroundness" in autism, particularly with regard to the poetry of Tito Mukhopadhyay, in his forthcoming book, *A Dispute with Nouns, or Adventures in Radical Relationality: Autism, Poetry, and the Sensing Body*.
23   Fernand Deligny, *Fernand Deligny Œuvres*, p. 600—trans. AM.

In his documentary film *Les Inconnus de la Terre*, the Italian film-maker Mario Ruspoli, a close friend of Tosquelles, describes his deep fascination with the Cévennes. To Ruspoli, the landscape appears to be an ancient world, eroded by the wind and weather and strewn with craters and caverns. He once called Mount Lozère, located in the Cévennes, the "most successful of all desolate landscapes that always looks good on postcards, like all such cold hells."[24] He added:

> Here one has to read between the roads. Above all, one must listen to the invisible whip. The ghost whip that blows 140 kilometers per hour—the wind. People cling tight to the granite between the wind and the silence. [...] Lozère is populated, not inhabited. The people of Lozère are born from the stone, to resist.[25]

Deligny wanted to document the lives of the neuro-diverse young people in the South—the "hibernation, the terraces, the stone-walled houses [...]."[26] The documentary film project was supposed to simply tell the story of these young people, living with one another, who set off to start their own life in the Cévennes. "How they organize their lives is the subject of the documentary."[27] Deligny's plan was to use the camera as a pedagogical tool. He wanted to film the experienced space via psychotic symptoms.

The milieu Deligny built up in the Cévennes consisted of networks that, in contrast to mainstream cinema, can be thought of as an anti-dote to concentration of power and identity, a way to avoid being "targeted." He broke off the project with Truffaut when, after the success of *Les 400 Coups*, Truffaut turned up with professional cameramen to work on *Le Moindre Geste*. Deligny felt as if the project was slipping away from him. Production resumed two years later, without Truffaut and his financial help.[28]

Josée Manenti, a young activist from the communist milieu of the French youth movement who met Deligny through her interest in the works of Tosquelles in Saint-Alban, made the resumption of *Le Moin-*

---

24 Mario Ruspoli quoted in François Bovier, "Regards sur l'"impouvoir": le 'cinéma direct' de Ruspoli, de la terre à l'asile," in: *Décadrages: Cinéma, à travers champs*, 18 (2011). Online: http://decadrages.revues.org/213 [accessed 30 December 2015]—trans. AM.

25 Ibid.

26 Sandra Álvarez de Toledo, "L'inactualité de Fernand Deligny," in: *Fernand Deligny Œuvres*, pp. 21–37—trans. AM.

27 Ibid.

28 Fernand Deligny, "Le Moindre Geste," p. 601.

dre Geste possible by making her own resources available. She bought herself a 16mm camera and an audio recorder. Manenti filmed the 16mm footage for *Le Moindre Geste* herself and thus became one of France's first female documentary camera operators. Her political and existential commitment, along with her artistic talent that co-authored the magical images in *Le Moindre Geste*, would have quickly catapulted her to fame. However, it was not until shortly before her death that her work was fully acknowledged in France.

Jean-Pierre Daniel, the film editor of *Le Moindre Geste*, described Manenti's appropriation of the camera as a physical process: "The camera was a machine that she discovered while shooting, and she found it to be very rigid and resistant."[29] Manenti adapted the camera to her needs. She experimented with shadow, the glistening light, and the landscape that was around the house. According to Deligny, her passion was "light and shadow, the slowness" and life "in the rhythm of the seasons."[30]

Her impact today can be interpreted as an example of commitment in a filmmaking and research collective, in which poetic force becomes a radical organizational principle for the method of research.

Camere

A few years later, when film footage of *Le Moindre Geste* was shown in La Borde, Deligny wrote to Truffaut to ask him for help in editing the film. He explained that it was not a film about "retarded" children but rather a study of the milieu. Milieu—a land before its territorialization—became the term for this sphere of action. In the milieu one fabricates the action of the plot as a creation of a cosmic relation. According to Deleuze and Guattari in *A Thousand Plateaus*, the milieu can be interpreted as the space between planes of consistency.

In order to understand autism and other forms of neuro-diversity, one has to give space to the experimental character of the exploration of the landscape itself. The possibility of seeing neuro-diverse actions in the proper context and within the environment depends on a creative act so that the mental space and the intentions of neuro-diverse actions can be intertwined with the project's organization itself.

---

29   Deligny/Jean-Pierre Daniel quoted in Josée Manenti, "Jo mon amie!" Online: http://www.polygone-etoile.com/files/images/2013/programmation2013/Jose-Manenti.pdf [accessed 12/30/2015]—trans. AM.

30   Fernand Deligny quoted in ibid.

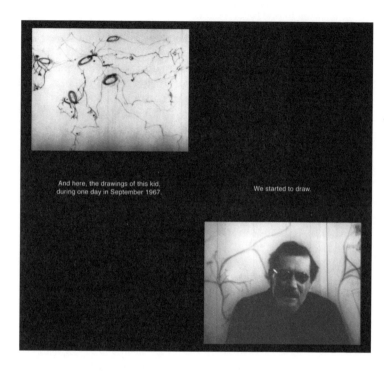

And here, the drawings of this kid, during one day in September 1967.

We started to draw.

Deligny wrote to Truffaut that they—the Research Group Deligny—had to invent this condition.

In 2006, after years of discontent, Manenti discussed her intentions with regard to *Le Moindre Geste* in conversation with the philosopher Henri Maldiney:

> I am, in talking about this film, in the same situation as the character. I found myself in front of a great, animated void, from where I was to discover and invent something. It was the invention of a gesture; a gesture invented from nothing. That is to say, it was a human invention par excellence, like the invention of the wheel or the invention of any scientific theory. This image of nothing, a nothing that is alive, a nothing that is animated through light—that was the thing that struck me the most when I started working on this film.[31]

---

31 Josée Manenti, "Ricochets du Moindre Geste" [2007], supplement to *Le Cinéma de Deligny* DVD (Paris: Éditions Montparnasse, 2007)—trans AM.

Nevertheless, the film *Le Moindre Geste* remains the collective success of a political and therapeutic movement that retreated into the deserted, rocky white limestone landscape of the Cévennes. Its poetic force met a surreal, preverbal ground, which presents itself as a micropolitical narrative about the smallest of gestures and about the language of things that, faced with the failure of words, recounts the landscape anew.

It became the cinema of the active power of images as an operative, living structure in opposition to the nominalism of representation and to the politics of signification. In contrast to the aspirations for a new objectivity in Germany, *Le Moindre Geste* places the intensification of affective dynamics through images at the level of the hyperreal in the space of the real, which is "realer than reality," as Tosquelles stated.

Translated by Angela Anderson and Vincent W.J. van Gerven Oei

Elisabeth von Samsonow

Latency: Biography of an Omniscient Spy

1.

"Nature loves to hide." *Heraclitus*

Designs of subjectivity and their reinvention, adjustment and oblit-eration depend on such an unmanageable abundance of parameters, paradigms, coordinates, and conditions that one cannot shake the impression that philosophy, the humanities and cultural sciences have enough material to delve into for years and years to come. Yana Milev recently explored the concept of *design anthropology* in a comprehen-sive publication,[1] a somewhat suspicious term that refers to the cir-cumstance that the human condition is pervaded by changing and arti-ficial programs and genomes that have a *design*. This *design* not only includes those elements of the cultural operating system that become effective via language, but also all approaches and actions interac-tively stabilized on molar and molecular levels.[2] Not least, *design* also includes the function of objects which dismantle subjective eccentric-ity/incompatibility with the world like gadgets or surrogates of *natural* objects that format and synchronize individuals. However, a contem-porary analysis of subjectivity is not only exacerbated by the sheer overabundance of parameters that need to be taken into consideration. That which may be defined as *symbolic* or sign-controlled politics has also either collapsed or became radicalized. Today, *designs* seem

---

1 See Yana Milev, *D.A.: A Transdisciplinary Handbook of Design Anthropology* (Bern: Peter Lang, 2013).

2 Regarding the question of *molecular* intervention, see also the latest debate in pharmacology by Paul B. Peciado and Bernhard Stiegler. Preciado refers directly to molecular medicine, primarily to the effects of hormones. See Paul B. Preciado, *Testo Junkie: Sex, Drugs, and Biopolitics in the Pharmacopornographic*, trans. Bruce Benderson (New York, N.Y.: Feminist Press, 2013). Stiegler, on the other hand, interprets the technological invasion by referring to the pharmacological model. See Bernhard Stiegler, *Ce qui fait que la vie vaut la peine d'être vecue: De la pharmacologie* (Paris: Flammarion, 2013); see also Ross Abinett, "The Politics of Spirit in Stiegler's Techno-Pharmacology." Online: http://tcs.sagepub.com/content/32/4/65.abstract, and Mark Featherstone, "Einstein's Nightmare: On Bernhard Stiegler's Techno-Dys-topia." Online: http://www.ctheory.net/articles.aspx?id = 728

hotwired to the subjects; their detour through spaces of symbolic order seems suspended. Therefore, the defrocked societies, which install *designs* in structures that are at least *ostensibly* horizontalized, find themselves increasingly placed in opposition to societies that equate religious views with their political maxims and cling to the extrapolation of signs. Abandoning the symbolic forces us to revise the real, which we must learn to recognize in its modulations. This new interest in the real is currently investigated in the disciplines of Speculative Realism, Object-Oriented Ontology, and Speculative Materialism,[3] all of them supported by economic connotations of the *real*, whose preferences are unequivocal. The reflexive reconstruction of Speculative Realism has brought into play the allegedly limitless validity of solipsistic, transcendental patterns of reasoning that acted like episodes of hallucinosis[4] and, in other words, destroyed or eclipsed the real. These philosophical tendencies can be characterized by their reference to a somewhat purist empirical concept of the real, which amounts to a metaphysical push-me-pull-me. Consequences of such approaches are, on the one hand, a defense against the Kantian analytics of transcendental philosophy, against postmodern and poststructuralist *critique* and, in consequence, the suppression of subject-orientated debates, in which some see a dangerous return of arbitrariness. Yet, a consolidation of these two routes—an object-driven *realistic* philosophy and a philosophy dealing with designs of subjectivity—would have been the truly important project here, in the matter of dissolving the schizoid powers of contemporary culture.

---

3 Reza Negarestani, *Cyclonopedia: Complicity with Anonymous Material* (Melbourne: Repress, 2008); Robin Mackay, "A Brief History of Geo Trauma," in: Ed Keller, Nicola Masciandaro, and Eugene Thacker, eds., *Leper Creativity Symposium* (New York, N.Y.: Punctum Books, 2012), p. 1–38; Ray Brassier, *Nihil Unbound. Enlightenment and Extinction* (London: Palgrave Macmillan, 2007); Quentin Meillassoux, *After Finitude. An Essay on the Necessity of Contingency*, trans. Ray Brassier (New York, N.Y.: Continuum, 2008); Robin Mackay, ed., *Collapse: Philosophical Research and Development*. Vol. VI: Geo/Philosophy (Falmouth: Urbanomic, 2010). Levi R. Bryant, *The Democracy of Objects* (Ann Arbor, Mich.: Open Humanities Press, 2011).
4 See also Hippoplyte Taine, *De l'intelligence* (Paris: Hachette, 1870), who argues that external perception is a *hallucination vraie*, a true hallucination. In this context, see also Eric Alliez's collaboration with Jean-Clet Martin, *L'oeil-cerveau. Nouvelles histoires de la peinture moderne* (Paris: Vrin, 2007). That which in Speculative Realism is termed *correlationism*—which is to say the reciprocal condition of cognition and the object of cognition—rests on the theory propagated since the nineteenth century that perception as an activity of specific bodies can only construct a modified image of the world. However, this theory, productive in aesthetics and art theory, plunged philosophical epistemologies into a crisis.

Contrary to today's overabundance of realism, which forebodes the transformation of the symbolic into *designs*, this chapter explores poetic concepts of the subject. I present a case study that illustrates how subjectivity emerges as a complex network of various commitments and how porous and dependent on definitions of its environment and parameters it remains. I show how the different possibilities gradually become manifest, how they liquefy again and how they can be used for economically, epistemologically, and gender-politically viable installations. My goal is to sketch a form of semiotico-cybernetic map searching for a utopian vector. The method remains doubly orchestrated and polyphonic; an operation that is based at once on a reconstruction of history and an anticipation of the future. When we speak of subjectivity, the time index (*earlier* = perfect tense; *later* = future tense) is only important to the extent that it refers to the interior structure of becoming and self-relation, as Eugen Fink has shown.[5] It is now as if this limitation that the symbolic exacts on the real opens up a space that allows for fictional interpretations of history in the first place, that is to say, narratives of interventions, shifts, and modifications that appear in the factual or the real without being themselves factual. In this context I take *fictional* to mean the effects of those artificial and *designed* elements that not only lift history out of natural history, but also, at least to a certain degree, deprive human cultures themselves of history, (re)turning it into mythology. It explains the lack of authorship in *discourse formation*, which is characterized by a network of various kinds of actors rather than by *authors*. A narrative recited in this fictional mode, having been written in the poetic past tense, then also sounds like a score of things to come. In it, history is the moment from where the narrative can be changed. Such paradoxical constellations exist not only on the poetic level of terminology in theoretical physics and its concepts of time, but also in philosophy, which gravitates towards the self-observation of the observed observer.

In order to get the philosophical terminology to liquefy—that is, to abandon its tendency towards petrification and historicization—the (prepositional) indexes DYS, TRANS, SYN, and INTER are used, acting—with a certain pretension that is specific to scientific jargon—as vectors of displacement, revision, expansion, and meta-navigation. They mark processes of preliminary disintegration, which accompany an increased liminal activity. Their hot zone is the threshold, the margin, of the prevailing fields. Hypothetical subjectivities emerge here,

---

5 Compare Eugen Fink, "Vergegenwärtigung und Bild. Beiträge zur Phänomenologie der Unwirklichkeit (I.Teil)," in: *Jahrbuch für Philosophie und phänomenologische Forschung*, XI (1930), p. 239–309.

which macerate political, logical, and social definitions—that is to say seemingly *private* or *individual* and, for example, sexual or gender definitions. The shift of previous lines within the vertical and horizontal coordinates has activated subjective fields to which one had not conceded subjectivity before and which now make high demands on the available criteria, categories, and terms. Countless re-constellations of competition, parallelism, congruence, and cooperation appear[6] in passing through all the various lines of species and technologies, which are hyper- and metabolically contextualized with one another in the concept of *universal nature*. This *universal nature* encompasses micro-worlds and macro-worlds and mediates among all of them and translates them into each other. They altogether mark not only the horizon of Being as a mega-object—the common place of coexisting and non-coexisting beings—but have to be defined as a pool of subjectivity to the highest degree. All deformations, transformations, and reformations which the dynamics of subjectivization entail, are considerable. Each new movement upsets the order in a productive way—alas, how great the excitement when a hitherto unknown subject type is introduced! The mood is comparable to that of witnessing the first UFO landing.[7] At the moment, we are noticing a considerable number of such shifts, but not the full extent of their active parameters. It seems as if new subjectivities do not even wait to be called on stage but get the audiences already fired up from behind the curtain.

Ecology and subject politics are combined on a broad basis with considerable euphoria. What this requires, according to Mick Smith, is "yet another Copernican revolution—a decentering, weakening, and overturning of the idea/ideology of human exceptionalism."[8] Reports of animals and plants that have become cognizant to represent their own subjectivities are still few and far between.[9] But it is fairly improb-

---

6 "Faced with such a situation, the first reaction we might have is that of the registrar, taking note of the many forms of being. Let's adopt ontography as a name for a general inscriptive strategy, one that uncovers the repleteness of units and their interobjectivity. From the perspective of metaphysics, ontography involves the revelation of object relationships without necessarily offering clarification or description of any kind." Ian Bogost, *Alien Phenomenology or What It's Like to Be a Thing* (Minneapolis, Minn.: University of Minnesota Press, 2012), p. 38.

7 Ian Bogost's *alien phenomenology* uses Graham Harman's and Alphonso Lingis's concept of carpentry, which explains "how things fashion one another and the world at large." Bogost, *Alien Phenomenology*, p. 93.

8 Mick Smith, *Against Ecological Sovereignty: Ethics, Biopolitics, and Saving the Natural World* (Minneapolis, Minn.: University of Minnesota Press, 2011), p. xii.

9 Ron Broglio, for instance, writes an unintentionally humorous introduction to his book *Surface Encounters: Thinking with Animals and Art*: "Properly, I should

able that the decentering of human beings would take place as a voluntary act of self-degradation. A variety of factors will have to converge: large-scale political and economic shifts, that is to say pressure to communicate and solve problems, as well as ludic drives, the dialectics of anti-structures, and so forth. The emergent type of subjectivity actually dominating the discussion is pan-democratic in a broader sense, trying to embrace a multispecies scenario; it becomes more and more inclusive, which goes well with Mick Smith's notion of the *weakening* of human exceptionalism. Smith opines that this weakening of the human position must necessarily lead to an erosion of sovereignty. He predicts a world in which a being-with-others produces an ecological community.[10] The will to acknowledge others as subjects—as equals—in an interface that is yet to be invented and constructed, provides the basis for such a future. In this endeavor human subjectivity, which may then no longer deserve this term, becomes *epidemic*. *Epidemic* means that information, bodies, capital, energy, and so on will circulate beyond the limits of one's own *demos*. It designs a structure presenting itself as an exo-hole or vortex. This is why *the epidemic* becomes both a logical and social category of interest. When Nicole Shukin uses the term *pandemic speculation* in her book *Animal Capital: Rendering Life in Biopolitical Times*, she means anything but a development of subjectivity. She refers to the use of this term in the study of infectious diseases and in opinion polls.[11] In my context, epidemic means that a subjectivity's validity is not, or does not remain, confined but instead expands—via contagions that are not necessarily viral or bacterial—*spills over* or migrates, in short: becomes rampant.

This is not to say that epidemic subjectivity is entirely new. Epidemic subjectivity already plays a role in ecological sovereignty, provided that the porousness of the human field is fully acknowledged.[12] Mick Smith

---

begin by thanking the animals. They, of course, will not recognize this thanks, nor particularly care about this book; nevertheless, without them and their alien agency, this book would not be possible." (Minneapolis, Minn.: University of Minnesota Press, 2011), p. xi.

10 Smith, *Against Ecological Sovereignty*, p. 208–209.

11 See chapter 4, "Biomobility. Calculating Kinship in an Era of Pandemic Speculation," in: Shukin, *Animal Capital*, pp. 181ff.

12 Mick Smith puts it this way: "How paradoxical, then, that a decision to (p)reserve some aspects of ecology, to maintain it in what is deemed to be its natural state, has today become a matter of political sovereignty. Paradoxical because, without all nature being initially assumed to be resource, there would be no original justification for political sovereignty: And yet, without political sovereignty, so the story now goes, nature cannot be preserved from being treated as a resource." Mick Smith, *Against Ecological Sovereignty*, p. xiii.

opines that the ideal of a group no longer governed by the privileged human subject would be realized in an "ecologically informed politics of 'anarcho-primitivism' that offers a fundamental critique of modern state authority and of human dominion over nature."[13] Smith's concept of primitivism is optimistic.[14] It is not the first time that a critique of civilization finds its salvation in its recourse to *primitive* societies. In the context of shifting and restructuring subjectivity, the specific knowledge and skills necessary to master the difficulties of new zones of encounter are suspected to be located in areas of highly situated knowledges.[15] We may thus assume expertise in indigenous societies and their *shamans*, which explains the current surge of shamanism in art and cultural sciences.

In the course of this revaluation of primitivism and shamanism, and with the introduction of terms such as animism and totemism,[16] the question arises as to how to deal with the methods of these *primitives*, whose competence emerges ever more clearly, in spite of the allegation that spiritually charged totemism represents a sheer anthropological fantasy. The devaluation of totemism that Lévi-Strauss caused in 1962 may well be irreversible, but there is still enough room for reinterpretation, as Philipp Descola has shown.[17]

There might be something like an everyday totemism, I argue, which we find in the most remote Brazilian rainforests as well as in highly civilized urban places. Totemism is useful for a contemporary analysis in that it assumes a kinship between members of different species. It is interesting both in a transgeneric—that is to say posthumanist—sense and in the context of media theory.[18] In contrast to animism, which, according to Descola, assumes a sharing of spiritual spaces without

---

13 Ibid, p. 70.
14 "Insofar as primitivists regard civilization as inherently and indeemably destructive, the scope of their critique is similarly all encompassing." Ibid, p. 71.
15 Donna Haraway coined this term in her seminal essay "Situated Knowledges: The Science Question in Feminism," *Feminist Studies*, vol. 14, no. 3 (Fall 1988), p. 575–599.
16 See also Philipp Descola, *Par-delà nature et culture* (Paris: Editions Gallimard, 2005). Descola adds the ethnographic category of naturalism and analogism to his analysis, thus expanding the canvas in a rather contemporary manner.
17 Claude Lévi-Strauss, *Le Totémisme aujourd'hui* (Paris: P.U.F., 1962). Jena-Paul Vernant's 1963 review of Lévi- Strauss's book is interesting in this context: Vernant refuses to acknowledge the effects of a totemism that has been debunked as a mere classification system or to admit "que l'animal, plus encore que 'bon à manger' est 'bon à penser.'" *Archives de Sociologie des Religions*, no. 16 (1963), p. 185.
18 See Elisabeth von Samsonow, Anti Electra. Totemism and Schizogamy, trans. Anita Fricek and Stephen Zepke (Minneapolis, Minn.: Univocal Publishing, 2017).

considering physical differences, totemism is particularly interested in the physical differences that would produce energetic tensions. I argue that the epidemic subject equals the totemic subject. The epidemic subject operates under the banner of the very subjective exo-expansion in which it is an expert. Totemic practice generalizes transgeneric communication as one person's or group's peculiar characteristic, as if to say, *There is (temporary unity) in our group, because we are related to an Other that has a different body.* The totemic subject is the alignment which, via the passage through other fields, actually (re)constructs the human field. Phase I is a regression suspending human generalism and exceptionalism. This is why the totemic subject equals the queer subject and the girl—as far as it is *pre- or posthuman* and *non-man.*

2.

The map that registers regional and transregional totemic acts has been updated by *animal studies*[19] and *alien phenomenology.* What has long been missing and is now occurring only rudimentarily, however, is a record of the seminal totemic event that would put Gaia—Earth itself—on the agenda.[20] In other words, we are to acknowledge that Earth would play an active role in the economy or interrelationality of subjectivities, that is to say we are to draw a transversal line through the horizons of human awareness, communication, production, gifts, trades, and so on in such a way that no single dot remains without relation to the line. This is a highly ambitious endeavor. But how to negotiate with Earth? How to speak with her? How to encounter this giant correlation?[21] Earth as an interlocutor must first be represented

---

19 See especially Donna Haraway, *When Species Meet* (Minneapolis, Minn.: University of Minnesota Press, 2008) and Nicole Shukin, *Animal Capital.*

20 James Lovelock deserves the honor of having put the *Gaia hypothesis* up for discussion, on which Bruno Latour recently based his new attempt of conceptualizing *Gaia.* See James Lovelock, *Gaia: A New Look at Life on Earth* (Oxford: Oxford University Press, 1979); Bruno Latour, "Waiting for Gaia. Composing the Common World through Art and Politics." Lecture at the French Institute in London 2011. Online: http://www.bruno.latour.fr/sites/default/124-GAIA-LONDON-SPEAP_0.pdf. See also the 2013 Gifford Lectures, available on Bruno Latour's website: Part One, "Facing Gaia" and "How to Make Sure Gaia is Not a God of Totality?" for the 2014 conference "Thousand Names of Gaia" in Rio de Janeiro: http://www.bruno.latour. fr/sites/default/files/138-THOUSAND-NAMES.pdf.

21 Timothy Morton succinctly described the problem in *Hyperobjects. Philosophy and Ecology after the End of the World* (Minneapolis, Minn.: Minnesota University Press, 2013).

by diplomatic envoys. This requires the opening of a *Gaian embassy* and with it, primarily, the election of a responsible representative who would *foretell and interpret* Gaia's intention. If we assume—as theology has always done—that every comprehensive awareness and every extensive form of subjectivity is an extrapolation towards divinity, then we must not only assume that Gaia represents an expanded and acute field of awareness, but also that she actively influences other, primarily less expanded and acute fields of awareness, as the economy of consciousness suggests. We might assume that Gaia herself delegates this to a suitable entity, to her representative, who ought to be able to speak other than human. But who might this delegate be? An individual that is to a sufficient extent an institution, a human being that is to a sufficient extent non-human, a vector that possesses sufficient subjectivity, a field that is to a sufficient extent a person. As Bruno Latour does not tire to point out, Gaia is an ancient mythological figure, one of the first Greek gods. Would it not make perfect sense to put an experienced *mystes* by her side, as a living principle, an interpreter, an oracle?[22]

Persephone might be assigned this task.[23] Persephone is already known as the one who accompanies Gaia as a mediator; she is the Gaia companion, the insider going back and forth from Hades. The agency would be, figuratively speaking, the revolutionary and violent *Anabasis of Persephone*, who stayed in *Katabasis* together with the Earth after the abduction.[24] Persephone is the Queen of the Underworld, she is latent or invisible like the biggest part of the Earth.[25] Both of them

22 See also Elisabeth von Samsonow, "Electra's Oracle: A Schizo-Geo-Analytical Account of Accelerationist Hyperstition," in: *Identities: Journal for Gender, Politics and Culture*, vol 12 (2015–2016), ed. Artan Sadiku, Institute for Social Sciences and Humanities (Skopje), p. 60–80.

23 See also Tatsuhiro Nakajima, „Ecopsychology of Demeter and Persephone: From Ancient Life of Eleusinian Mystery to Postmodern Bio-Politics of Fukushima Nuclear Disaster," in: *International Journal of Jungian Studies*, vol. 7, no. 3 (London: Routledge, 2015), p. 194–205.

24 See also Hollie Jean Hannan, *Initiation Through Trauma. A Comparative Study of the Descents of Inanna and Persephone (Dreaming Persephone Forward)*, (open source: UMI, 2008).

25 The topos of the invisible body was virulent in poststructuralism and has remained so until today, as for instance in Rosi Braidotti's recommendation: "Rethinking the embodied structure of human subjectivity after Foucault, I would recommend that we take as the starting point the paradox of the simultaneous overexposure and disappearance of the body in the age of postmodernity." Rosi Braidotti, "Teratologies" in: Ian Buchanan and Claire Colebrook, eds., *Deleuze and Feminist Theory* (Edinburgh: Edinburgh University Press, 2001), p. 158, see also Chapter II: "Enfleshed Communities."

are cryptic and under-cover. An invisible diplomat is a spy in relation to the group she has to communicate with and bring her message forth. The invisible diplomat is the subject that makes the agenda of Earth most clearly visible. The spy is the subject transferring the Earth's symptoms. She is Earth's billboard. At the moment, it seems, she is still partially invisible. As anabasis advances, they will both *come out.*

The subjection of Earth as portrayed in the Bible limited the acts of creation to God and, on a smaller scale, to human beings. *Subjection of Earth* is synonymous with the *becoming-latent* of the Earth, which was produced by a type of withdrawal of subjectivity known from colonialist records. Decolonizing Earth, the end of her *below*, demands a revision of all previous categories of thought. If philosophy was once metaphysics—and primarily cosmology at that—the process that would be required is re-cosmologizing thought that returns to a decolonialized Earth its rightful place. What would be novel about this in comparison to the older cosmologies is the hypothesis that thought is geo-logically affected. It not only constructively grasps the cosmos, but symptomatizes it. Bruno Latour called this the synchronicity of "Gaia-in-us" and "us-in-Gaia."[26] This structure cannot be articulated by means of current philosophical models. Therefore, it requires finding a way to reflexively survey the impact of Earth on thought itself, which is to say its Earth requirement. With this omen, human thought is outbid by Earth subjectivity. This marks the end of pure spirit and the beginning of the *oracle.* Thought takes place under the conditions of the Earth; its form is *earthbound.*

If we eventually envisage an *end of the below*, of Earth's dystopia, we might speak of its resurrection instead of its anabasis. This term, however, might put us on the wrong track, because we may again see some *higher spirit* brought into play. The philosophical feat now, as Bruno Latour has so lucidly seen, is to avoid re-theologizing in the old style. In doing so, we need to consult the tablet of the major types of subjectivity in order to outline *Earth awareness*, or the subject of Earth as a first thing in philosophy, and get at least a preliminary sketch of it.

An ascent after the descent into the underworld—*emergence* after latency, a move towards the manifest—that is the dialectic materialism of Earth. The return of Earth in the guise of a *subject* is illustrated by the anabasis (Greek for "ascent") of Persephone, by ending dystopia and crypto-subjectivity. Strangely, this return introduces the motif of the *end of history* into human things at the very moment there is a

---

26 See Bruno Latour, "Waiting for Gaia," p. 10.

beginning of the history of Earth that is no longer mere geography or geology. To the same extent that a new subject type arises (a "secular goddess Gaia," as Bruno Latour puts it), there is also a new object type to emerge. Since the revaluation that object-oriented ontology has provided for the object is geared towards endowing things with subjectivity, Timothy Morton's discussion of the "new Earth" and its mega-features ("hyper-objectivity") can for all intents and purposes be equated with Bruno Latour's "Gaia" project in his "Gaia Lectures." Here, finally, utmost planetary object-likeness and utmost subject status converge.

Persephone constitutes the symbolic person who embarks on a quest to understand Earth from within. She is the specialist epidemically infecting others via her totem. Earth's new status as a subject can be modeled in a similar fashion by way of a subject-dynamic equivalence that would tie together Earth and Persephone. Persephone would be the particular gadget tracking Gaia, performing their parallel transgression, a transition that serves to bring the crucial message: Subjectivity exists outside the realm of what has thus far been imaginable. Persephone goes to the underworld and becomes an insider. As long as this underworld was only identified geotopically, which is to say as inorganic, it wasn't given much credit and attention. Persephone became dystopian not only in space and time but also epistemologically. This dystopia describes *Earth oblivion*, the negative Earth career or Earth's latency, which has to be considered with Hannah Arendt's *birth oblivion* in mind. On a planet that is itself a complex mega-topos, *dystopia* is a real problem. Persephone's Katabasis, or becoming latent, hence refers to a fracture in Earth's topology, a fracture in its becoming, which should have been somehow repaired by the heroes' and heroines' descent—from Persephone to *Faust II*.

But how can the body of a planet that is topos-for-existences have such a *fracture*, a crack in its identity? How did this happen? What has occurred that this body is not simple expression or epiphany, pure manifestation, pure expressive surface? What kinds of occurrences do we have to suppose in order to arrive at this inconsistency on a planetary scale? Who or what is the eventual originator of this drama? Does Earth suffer its inhabitants' colonial disregard and their lust for destruction? What is going on here?

Arguably the most important question is that of how exactly Gaia's subjectivity field is connected with the body of Earth. Does the same apply to Earth that applies to the living bodies on or in it—that the sort of absolute identity which the coincidence of body and subjectivity implies is untenable, and only preliminary, biologically, culturally, and technologically conveyed designs of identity and syntheses exist that are only *relatively* stable? What might the nature of this event be that makes Earth's body vibrate in such a way that Gaia appears amidst the physics of gasses, volcanoes, mineral formation, and meteorology? What body does Earth have? Are we to regard DYS, TRANS, SYN, and INTER bodies as political bodies in which this experimental event of the bodies' and subject fields' coming-to are performed as a planetary drama?

It is difficult enough to describe Earth's coming-to as a (subject-) metaphysical event affecting all remaining subjectivity. It is more difficult still to revise the basic conditions of production and capital under these conditions. Where Marx used "nature" and "matter" as abstracts, Earth is now used, provided it is she who is becoming not only a materialist signifier but an actor in an economy that has expanded to become ecology. The immanent transformation of philosophy builds on the absolute priority and universalization of the category of inside and interior and the extension of the subject zone, which results in endless shifts in all structures. Earth represents a *dea abscondita*, a pagan version of the hidden God, whose exhumation as treasure— for example as *Rare Earth*—has long begun. In this sense, the German *Bodenschatz* (natural resources, literally: earthly treasure) defines natural gas, crude oil, coal, gold, aluminum, and all other metals such as platinum, precious and semi-precious stones, and rare earth elements (Promethium, Thulium, and so on) occurring in the ground. It is needless to mention that the natural resources are the main factors of contemporary economy and, therefore, contemporary politics. Mining such natural resources approximates a Katabasis, an inspection of the interior, so that we can at least determine that drilling, carving, and mining perform the same spatial movement as Persephone in her descent.[27]

If the primacy of Earth applies, the requisites of embodiment are different from those under the primacy of humans, established and enforced on a global scale. If Earth is set as the body within which all bodies are to be understood as derived and synthesized bodies— that is to say as inter-dependent earth products or earthlings—then this *being-in* results in a series of conclusions, from which we may, in turn, reshape economic circulation. Earth, then, relates to human beings, who have thus far at best been illustrated by way of the sun's relation to Earth—in a relation of asymmetrical abundance, which, as Jean-François Lyotard put it, no human potlach could possibly counterbalance. This asymmetrical correlation is epidemic.

---

27 In this context, see Reza Negarestani's wonderful discussion of the "(w)hole complex" in *Cyclonopedia*.

3. Give and Take: Epidemic Circulation

The anabasis of Persephone changes the economy and turns it upside down. Dystopia of life produces dependence, lack, guilt/debt. In order to get a sense of the features of the utopian Gaia economy, we might look at the transversal line that Persephone draws in the fields of not only subjectivity but also of *things*—bodies, objects, goods, commodities, and so forth. Is Gaia a trap, a torture rack, a debtor's prison? Or is she a benevolent host and resource? If we consider the principle of the gift and of hospitality, we might investigate the function of balance and fantasize about a kind of hospitality without obligations of any kind. Structuralism had thrown its resources into the notion of the gift because of its glorious paired symmetries, which, compliant to the rules, at times could be annulled, thwarted, or twisted in order to return to the very paired symmetries with which it started out. What if one started with an asymmetry from the outset, what if one had the circulation of life, bodies, goods, and signs that make up the economy, be founded on an act in which asymmetry is inherent insofar as the giver, the donor, the supplier, the producer is greater, more substantial, and entirely different? Human economy on a global scale consists in a continuous act of taking in which asymmetry is inherent from the outset. This is not fatal as long as we are allowed to assume that this first act of giving is carried out without calculation, without resentment, without remorse, without intent to commit. Thus far, every form of economy has introduced a gift that serves to arrest the receivers of the gift, to put them in chains, to make them bleed. Blessed are those who give. But cursed are those who take. Even Jacques Derrida had doubts about whether there could be such a thing as an unpoisoned gift.[28]

The suspicion that wastefulness serves the purpose of letting one walk into the trap of duty and debt is therefore in some way justified. How did the act of giving grow this thorn? To the extent that asymmetrical abundance has been overwritten and veiled by exploitation, manufacture, and industry—its origins refined or canceled by refining them—the synthetic principle of production and manufacture has taken the place of the principle of giving. The consequences are well-known. For women—who, for reasons not yet fully spelled out, had been added to the side of the Great Giver—this circumstance boded ill, because the unconscious or organic pact they had symbolically made with the Earth in terms of proliferation caused them to become some-

---

28 Compare Jacques Derrida, *Given Time: I. Counterfeit Money*, trans. Peggy Kamuf, (Chicago, Ill.: Chicago University Press, 1992).

what latent *with* her. A truly mysterious event. Tentative interpretations include: an intervention by the principle of power and the effects of its accumulative, veiling nature that distorts ownership structures; geo-traumas and, consequently, the repression and disfigurement of Earth as *paradise*; the obstruction of *sink marks* in operations *à la* anti-nature = culture, which resulted in some well-known encroachments on the human field (demons, false gods, despots, and puppets of all kinds). Disturbing the alliance with the asymmetrical abundance triggers competition, lack, and competitive accumulation: territorial and *population-related* infringements, the amassment of treasures, a pursuit of influence and wealth, the creation of the *global North*.

Giving without intention, without manipulation, without will to obligation is unthinkable, which explains this thorn, this allegation of resentment that is modeled after the supposedly cunning and devious snake of paradise, who hands Eve the apple. However, if, as I have indicated, Earth is put on the philosophical agenda as a subject, if Earth becomes recognizable as a navigating context, how could we possibly get any idea other than that this is yet another manipulative act? How to place it on the philosophical horizon, if the signs point to betrayal and manipulation? Can we admit that Earth has subjectivity before it has its justification, secured in a kind of *geodicy*? Does an Earth that has thus far been latent perhaps bear an unknown problem that has less to do with human beings and their defective cognition than with the history of Earth itself? Must we not recognize this problem and shelve it for good first, before we set about proclaiming a new eco-romanticism? How to peel Earth from the spell of the creation narrative, which has turned it into the planet of crime and punishment?

Moreover, are we allowed to let her return so *disfigured*, as a trauma generator? Who is to blame for such a terrifying Earth, and how and why is Earth to blame for us? Earth-latency as a diagnosis is so general that Pierre Klossowski, for instance, fantasized about the "absolute owner" in *Living Currency*: "Who is this absolute owner? The 'divinity,' or 'inexhaustible life' [...]."[29] This life, which is given by the absolute owner, has *no price*.[30] The inexhaustible gift of the absolute owner is accepted, provided the capacity to receive exists, whereas—and that is the point—no-one can receive more than "he is capable of giving—or else he will end up belonging to whoever he continues ceaselessly to

---

29 Pierre Klossowski, *Living Currency*, trans. Jordan Levinson. Online: http://anticoncept.phpnet.us/Livingcurrency.htm (accessed June 29, 2016), trans. into German as *Die lebende Münze* by Martin Burckardt (Berlin: Kulturverlag Kadmos, 1998), p. 64.

30 Ibid.

receive from."[31] The conclusion: "He who gives and does not receive takes possession, every time, of he who, having *received in order to be*, cannot give; the latter is wholly given over in advance to a power that increases instead of diminishing by giving without receiving, and thus can *take back more* than it had given."[32]

This compulsory prescription of *receiving without alternative* adds up to a debt gulag on a massive scale, to the enslavement of the receivers, who are incapable of repayment. Like life like the rest—that is to say: like the absolute owner, like all the others. In this notion, capitalism and industrialized production are perceived as the inevitable image of the first economic conditions, where there are only Danaan gifts. But again: Where does this assumption originate? Why does Klossowski—and incidentally also Lyotard and Bataille—insist on the idea that receiving life inevitably leads to a constitutive debt? If this rule applies then it is clear that "[i]n the world of industrial manufacturing, what's attractive is no longer what appears naturally to be for free, but the price put on what is naturally for free."[33] The lie consists in the fact that we always assume a normative symmetry that can never be one.

4. Asymmetrical Abundance

I take an asymmetry as a starting point, too, but assess it differently. I claim that the negative asymmetry of destructive giving belongs to the era of Earth-latency, belongs to crypto-Earth. The one described above, the one that led to the enslavement of the gift receiver, was the asymmetrical negative interdependence, of which Maurizio Lazzarato's text *The Making of the Indebted Man* provides an in-depth analysis.[34] For Lazzarato, it is credit, which is to say the gift, that must be surpassed with interest in restitution; otherwise the threat of degeneration to the service, the loss, looms large again. Interestingly, Klossowski indeed conceives of the gift of the absolute owner as credit, through which negative asymmetry is established. Much like latency and manifestation refer to another, negative asymmetry is contrasted with the model of asymmetrical abundance. It is only at this point that we notice a significant rupture between the order of Gaia and the order of capital. Asymmetrical abundance means that the gift of the absolute owner,

31 Ibid., p. 67.
32 Ibid., p. 65.
33 Ibid.
34 Maurizio Lazzarato, *The Making of the Indebted Man: An Essay on the Neoliberal Condition*, Trans. Joshua David Jordan (Los Angeles, CA: Semiotext(e), 2012).

who this time is *Gaia*, is given to us, as if from an absolute source without limits, without constituting debt, without obligation that could be augmented to the point of slavery—we might also say: we happen *on* it, we are attributed with it, we obtain it. Here, the coefficient is inversely proportional to that of debt, which wants what was given to be returned with interest. In the case of asymmetrical abundance, 1 becomes 10, which constitutes the approximate average proliferation rate across all species.

The history of terra-economy or territorial economy, whose exchange and trade were preceded by this principle of asymmetrical abundance, tells the story of how Persephone descends *into the Earth*. As long as Persephone abides in her dystopia—so the story goes—Demeter refuses to let anything grow. While Demeter is sulking, growth is projected exclusively onto capital. The Earth's and Persephone's biographies stay connected. The instant Persephone returns, growth is restored; the economy of abundance emerges, *geo-luxury*. The story has it that Persephone's descents and ascents took place cyclically—annually or twice a year. Assuming the *displaced* connection of asymmetrical abundance in the *displaced person* of Persephone yields an instructive picture. This girl is a walking seismograph gadget depicting the abundance of terrestrial production and its proliferation rates in human production or generation. The girl itself is the symbol of asymmetry and, interestingly, she is the symbol of both versions of economic asymmetry: She is the symbol of asymmetrical abundance inasmuch as she brings life to Earth from the earth as a reverse Prometheus (or his counterpart), but she also becomes the symbol of perverted, negative asymmetry planted into manufacturing, industrial, and capitalist processes as a driving force of the system or *living currency*, as an allure, a promise, a reminder, a decoy, as kidnapped energy. Introducing her into negative asymmetry as shimmering bait stabilizes the context of theft, which turns abundance into credit. Asymmetrical abundance is planted in the girl, and because she is supremely suitable as a victim or symbolic resource, she is called to serve the negative asymmetry of the context of debt as well. In their horrible book about girls, Tiqqun only saw this one side of the coin.[35] Tellingly, Klossowski notes that workers could very well have expected to be paid in girls.[36]

---

35 Tiqqun, *Preliminary Materials for a Theory of the Young-Girl*, trans. Ariana Reines (Los Angeles, Calif.: Semiotext(e), 2012).

36 "How can a human 'person' serve the function of currency? How could producers, instead of 'paying for' women, ever get paid 'in women'? How would businessmen and industrialists pay their engineers and workers, then? 'In women.'" Pierre Klossowski, *Living Currency*.

5. The Anabasis of the Monstrous Girl: Lara-Croftian Ontology

The anabasis of the girl, her *escape*, begins the very moment Earth returns not only as a philosophical object, but as a subject.[37] The shortage of resources, the energy question, the inflationary production of human beings—all these things that are connected to devaluation and indebtedness—change against the background of asymmetrical abundance. The appropriation of *production* in industrial and post-industrial capitalism makes visible that it always only transforms, rearranges, and synthesizes in a secondary production (not reproduction!), on the condition that the proliferation of Gaia be veiled. Poststructuralism's *simulacrum* and its destructive omnipotence disintegrate, even without the heroic attack by Speculative Materialism, in the moment in which the theft and mockery of abundance that logically followed from the latency of Gaia, are exhibited. The figure of the girl is the *hot figure*, because the lines cross in her in such a way that she both *has access* and *acts as access*, like a totemic apparatus or virus. Persephone's anabasis is synchronized with the (re)creation of Earth as a subject; the girl, Persephone, is the representative, the spokesperson, the Earth telephone. Her monstrous reference is twofold: on the one hand, to *Earth* as her oracle and, at the same time, to the human field as a totemic operator gifted with epidemic competence. Her *schizosomatic* position repairs the economic context motivated by theft. The words of Stendhal and Nietzsche—"Those who can't find a way to give themselves freely find a way to sell themselves," and "No one wants her for free, so she has to sell herself!"[38]—are definitively to be corrected: "No one can pay ever for her anymore, so she gives herself freely."

Translated by Georg Bauer

---

37 See Margot K. Louis, *Persephone Rises 1860–1927: Mythography, Gender and the Creation of a New Spirituality* (Farnham: Ashgate, 2009).
38 Klossowski, *Living Currency*.

Contributors

Arantzazu Saratxaga Arregi is a Ph.D. candidate in Philosophy and Media Theory at the University for Arts and Design, Karlsruhe. She is working on her proposal of a 'matrix' theory, which she has been developing in her Ph.D. project. She has given several lectures and seminars on questions of matrixial philosophy and has translated several German philosophers into Spanish. She teaches Media Theory at the Freiburg College of Art, Design and Popular Music. Currently, she is working on an essay entitled "The Polyvalence of Matrixial Symbolism: On the Philosophical Tie of Ontogeny in the Work of Goethe."

Johanna Braun holds a MFA and Ph.D. from the Academy of Fine Arts Vienna. The emphasis of Braun's academic and artistic research lies on the girl's symbolic urgency in relation to media philosophy, US-American literature, film and television studies, and its intermediality.

Levi R. Bryant is Professor of Philosophy at Collin College in Frisco, Texas. He is the author of *Difference and Givenness: Deleuze's Transcendental Empiricism and the Ontology of Immanence* (2008), *The Democracy of Objects* (2011), *Onto-Cartography: An Ontology of Machines and Media* (2014) and the editor, with Graham Harman and Nick Srnicek, of *The Speculative Turn: Continental Materialism and Realism* (2010).

Francesca Coin is Professor of Sociology at Ca' Foscari University of Venice, where she teaches Neoliberal Policies and Global Social Movements. She is the Director of the Institute in Austerity, Society and the Commons at the Global Center for Advanced Studies. She has published extensively on the relationship between finance, labor and subjectivity, drawing particularly on the work of Marx, Nietzsche and Deleuze to undo the notion of subjectivity in the neoliberal world. Currently, she is based in Athens where she is doing research on the impact of austerity on life in Greece. The tension between austerity and the commons is the topic of her latest book, *Non salvateci più—'Οχι άλλο σώσιμο* (2016).

Karin Ferrari is a visual artist based in Vienna. She uses visual material from pop culture, focusing on an aesthetic vocabulary that is produced collectively on the internet and linked to a body of knowledge and aesthetic that has emerged on YouTube on the intersection of academic theory, (political) paranoia, and fantasy fiction. Her web series, *DECODING (THE WHOLE TRUTH)*, has been a success on YouTube. The videos examine TV clips and music videos in order to reveal hidden messages.

Boyan Manchev is Professor of Philosophy at the New Bulgarian University, Guest Professor at HZT Berlin and former Program Director and Vice President of the International College of Philosophy in Paris. His main areas of research include ontology, political philosophy, and philosophy in art. Recent publications include *The Body-Metamorphosis* (2007), *L altération du monde: Pour une esthétique radicale* (2009), *La Métamorphose et l'instant: Désorganisation de la vie* (2009), and *Logic of the Political* (2012).

Angela Melitopoulos is an artist and Professor at the Royal Academy of Fine Arts Copenhagen. She has produced numerous films and has published articles, both formats realized in close collaboration with the sociologist and philosopher Maurizio Lazzarato. Her main research interests are migration, mobility, collective memory in relation to geography and media representation, and archives. Her work received several awards and was shown in numerous international festivals, exhibitions, and museums such as the Generali Foundation Vienna, the Berlinale, the Haus der Kulturen der Welt, the Antoni Tàpies Foundation Barcelona, the KW Institute for Contemporary Art in Berlin, the Manifesta 7, the Centre Georges Pompidou in Paris, and the Whitney Museum of American Art in New York.

Suzana Milevska is a curator and theorist of art and culture. Her projects focus on the postcolonial critique of identity politics and the hegemonic power regimes of representation at the intersection of gender, ethnicity, race, and sexuality. She was a Fulbright Senior Research Scholar and has a Ph.D. in Visual Cultures from Goldsmiths, University of London. In 2010, she published *Gender Difference in the Balkans* and edited *The Renaming Machine: The Book*. She was the Endowed Professor for Central and South Eastern European Art Histories at the Academy of Fine Arts Vienna and a visiting professor at the Visual Culture Unit at the Vienna University of Technology (2013–15).

Elisabeth von Samsonow is Professor of Philosophical and Historical Anthropology at the Academy of Fine Arts Vienna, Austria, and an artist and curator. She is a member of GEDOK Munich, was the Artistic Director of the Neubeurer Woche (2011–2014), and produces a philosophical TV show, *STUDIO ELEKTRA* (Okto TV). Her recent publications include *Anti-Elektra: Totemismus und Schizogamie* (2007, trans. into French by Béatrice Durand as *L'anti-Electre: Totémisme et schizogamie*, Metis Presses Genève 2015; trans. into English by Anita Fricek and Stephen Zepke as *Anti-Electra. Totemism and Schizogamy*, Univocal Publishing Minneapolis 2017), *Egon Schiele: Ich bin die Vielen* (2010), *Egon Schiele: Sanctus Franciscus Hystericus* (2012).

Peter Sloterdijk wrote his Ph.D. thesis on *Literature and the Organization of Life Experience. Theory and History of Autobiography in the Weimar Republic 1918–1933* under the supervision of Klaus Briegleb in 1976. Between 1978 and 1980, Sloterdijk resided in the ashram of Bhagwan Shree Rajneesh in the Indian city of Poona and has been working as a freelance writer since the 1980s. His book, *Kritik der zynischen Vernunft*, published by Suhrkamp in 1983 and translated into English as *Critique of Cynical Reason* in 1988, is one of the bestselling philosophical books of the twentieth century. From 2001 to 2015, Sloterdijk was the director of the Karlsruhe University of Arts and Design.